CAROLE TARLINGTON / WENDY MICHAELS

BUILDING PLAYS

Simple playbuilding techniques at work

Heinemann
Portsmouth, NH

34743970

© 1995 **Pembroke Publishers**
538 Hood Road
Markham, Ontario, Canada L3R 3K9

Published in the United States of America by
Heinemann
A division of Reed Elsevier Inc.
361 Hanover Street, Portsmouth, NH 03801-3912
ISBN (U.S.) 0-435-08689-8

Canadian Cataloguing in Publication Data

Tarlington, Carole
  Building plays: simple playbuilding techniques
at work

Includes bibliographical references and index.
ISBN 1-55138-053-6

1. Drama in education.   I. Michaels, Wendy.
II. Title.

PN3171.T37 1995   792'.071'2   C95-931400-8

A catalogue record for this book is available from the British
Library.
Published in the U.K. by
Drake Educational Associates
St. Fagan's Road, Fairwater, Cardiff CF5 3AE

Editor: Joanne Close
Design: John Zehethofer
Cover photography: Ajay Photographics
Typesetting: Jay Tee Graphics Ltd.

This book was produced with the generous assistance of the
government of Ontario through the Ministry of Culture and
Communications.

Printed and bound in Canada by Webcom
9 8 7 6 5 4 3 2 1

Contents

Acknowledgments

The authors wish to thank the following people:

- Juliana Saxton, Wendy Grant and Heather Hall for valuable feedback on the manuscript.
- John Sereda for his music for "Immigrant Stories" and his permission to reprint the lyrics of his songs in this book
- Andy Goodyear for his practical help
- Richard Barrett and Owen Hardy for their inspiration.

AND

The many young actors from both Sydney and Vancouver schools and the actors from the Vancouver Youth Theatre and the Shakespeare Globe Centre, Australia, who taught us a lot about Playbuilding.

Introduction

What Is Playbuilding?

The room buzzes with excitement as twenty young actors aged twelve to sixteen work together in small groups. They negotiate, try out ideas, analyze, evaluate, modify plans, and practise. There is laughter, argument, and intensity as ideas are refined, reworked, and practised again. The teacher/director circulates, asking questions, making suggestions, and providing encouragement. There is thinking, enjoyment, and learning happening in this lively room. What is going on here? Playbuilding, of course.

Playbuilding is a unique method of working with groups of actors to create a play. Unlike writing a play or rehearsing a play that has been written by a playwright, playbuilding is a collaborative venture that involves the entire group in the creative process. Collaboration occurs in both the developing of the script and the performing of the final product.

Playbuilding is hard work – all building is – but it is also rewarding and creative, involving all members of the group in a unique process. Because group size is irrelevant (it is possible to playbuild with three actors or thirty), the method is of particular interest to teachers and others who want to take the ideas of a group and express them in dramatic form. Age is not a factor – we have playbuilt successfully with people of all ages, from five to sixty five.

Playbuilding is enjoyable and invigorating. As people come together to explore an issue or idea, they find themselves drawn into a process that allows for all views of the world. This process represents a voyage of discovery in which everyone can learn and benefit. As group members engage in playbuilding, they become involved in a venture of creativity.

Playbuilt plays are powerful. Each member of the group contributes in some way to the development of the presentation; the final performance reflects the creativity and energy of all its members. Different people bring different perspectives and skills to the process – all of this input can be assimilated into the structure of the play.

Actors involved in a playbuilt play take ownership in a special way. Since the final play reflects the views and voices of all group members, there is enormous individual and collective satisfaction and a sense of having created an artistic piece. The playbuilt play reinforces the idea that we are all creative beings, that everyone has ideas, and that collectively we are strong.

Playbuilding demonstrates clearly that plays and playmaking are not the domain of a few "arty" people. Great plays are about people like us. Our lives, thoughts, and ideas are as valid as those of any published playwright. The notion that playwrights write because they have something to say is often foreign to people whose only experience of drama has been playing an elf in the grade one end-of-year play. Unfortunately, many of the plays in school anthologies are not written because a playwright has something important to say; instead, they are written to help teachers meet the expectations of parents who want to see their child on stage in a drama production. Many teachers are aware of the inadequacy of these plays, but believe themselves unable to improve on these rather weak standbys.

Learning how to manage playbuilding will allow teachers to "put something on" at Christmas, or at the school assembly if that is what is required. More importantly, however, a teacher's familiarity with playbuilding ensures that the young actors in his or her charge will have taken part in a creative, stimulating, and meaningful learning experience. Audiences watching a playbuilt performance recognize the immediacy of the actors' involvement and belief in the play, which adds to its impact. This is what playbuilding does. This is what theatre is for.

What this Book Offers Readers

This book explores playbuilding through the presentation of a number of projects with students of varying ages in a variety of contexts. Some of the plays described were created in Australia, others in Canada. All were successful, and the young people involved in them learned, worked hard, and gained satisfaction from presenting to an audience. Although this book focuses on practical components of managing playbuilding, it also offers a theoretical framework for playbuilding and analyzes the type of learning that occurs in playbuilding.

The plays outlined in this book are, for the most part, theme plays. They do not centre on a main character, but rather on the actors ' reactions to, and ideas about, a particular theme. For readers interested in developing other kinds of playbuilt plays, we refer you to Errol Bray's excellent book, *Playbuilding* (Currency Press, Australia).

The descriptions contained in this book are not intended to serve as lesson plans. They reflect our experiences with groups of young people in a specific context. Readers of this book will not get the same response since the groups they work with will have unique reactions to the techniques and methods presented. It is our hope that you will take the ideas described in this book and adapt them to create your own playbuilding approaches.

This book can be used by anyone – elementary school teacher, high school teacher, or youth worker – regardless of the amount of past experience with drama. The methods described in this book will enable you to explore relevant topics with young people while at the same time build their self-esteem and ability to work as part of a group. As an additional aid, we have included a comprehensive glossary of terms since drama/theatre terminology tends to differ from country to country.

The excitement and sense of achievement from creating a playbuilt play is tangible. Young people display enthusiasm, focus, and commitment when involved in playbuilding projects; they learn, grow, and become more self-confident. As well, they recognize the value of the process in their learning. This awareness is expressed in the following evaluation, written by an adolescent after her first experience with playbuilding.

"I had never been in a real play before (just ones already written) and I can't believe how much I learned in just two weeks, not just about acting, but how plays are created and lots about myself and the other kids in the group. This play is ours and it told the audience about things we think are important. It was really hard work, but so much fun. It was excellent that we could do this in just two weeks. I was amazed. Playbuilding is radical. Let's do more."

Sarah, aged fifteen

Yes, let's!

1

What can be learned from playbuilding

Learning Experiences and Playbuilding

Playbuilding is a rich approach to drama that encompasses learning experiences in a number of areas including theatre, human behavior, presenting ideas, co-operating, thinking, research, and the pursuit of excellence.

THEATRE

Playbuilding offers participants the opportunity to learn a great deal about how theatre works, and to acquire a broad spectrum of theatre skills. During the process, participants work as playwrights, actors, directors, audience members, designers, critics and technicians, and have the opportunity to see, at close range, how a writer/dramaturge and director/designer work. In many school plays, however, one person may fill several roles.

Participants learn how plays are structured and gain an understanding of the discipline and commitment needed to create and perform a theatre piece. As actors, they learn to use and control their voices and bodies. They gain confidence, and experience the joy of creating work that can be shared with an audience.

HUMAN BEHAVIOR

Theatre is about human relationships. To build a play, it is necessary to explore human behavior and analyze various points of view. During playbuilding, group members define their attitudes and explore other points of view, leading them to new understandings regarding human behavior.

Since theatre is presentational, actors learn many techniques for presenting ideas. These techniques include: naturalistic scenes, monologues, mime, movement, dance, choral work, slapstick comedy, satire, and song.

The playbuilding process requires that ideas be explored through these techniques and be reshaped and refined before they are presented to an audience. Thus actors learn to manipulate the infinite ways of presenting ideas through enactment and performance while learning to make judgments about which technique is most effective in a given situation.

CO-OPERATION

Playbuilding, in order to be successful, must be a co-operative and collaborative process. Each playbuilding group must work together to sort ideas, negotiate, and reach conclusions that are agreeable to all members of the group.

THINKING

The playbuilding process requires rigorous thinking on the part of all group members. It ensures that participants think of verbal, visual, and movement aspects of a play – discussion and questioning by the writer/director help participants to think in all three modes.

Actors working in playbuilding constantly think of new ideas, and make and test hypotheses. Many of these ideas must be translated into other forms to ensure group understanding. Regardless of how an idea develops, many will give rise to sometimes heated discussion. Before the group can move on, a contentious idea must be worked through and acceptable compromises made.

As in any collaborative process, listening is a crucial component. Participants in playbuilding must be ready to listen to another's ideas, consider them, and if agreed to by all, developed as part of the play. Since the group will utilize non-naturalistic techniques, the ability to observe and critically read messages conveyed by visual and movement modes of expression is also important.

Analysis and evaluation are central to playbuilding, as decisions concerning presentation of ideas occurs throughout the process. The decision of whether it would be best to present an idea through a scene, monologue, or movement must be made in the context of the whole play, the performance space, and the skills and interests of the group. Actors must develop skills in analysis. Sometimes, seemingly good ideas must be discarded – the group must make those difficult decisions with the best interests of the play at heart.

RESEARCH

Research is vital to any playbuilding project. First, members must focus on identifying questions central to the theme of the play. Second, they must ask themselves two basic questions: what they want or need to know about the question, and what sources will most efficiently supply them with answers.

Research can involve "looking it up in the library" or conducting interviews with both group members and people outside the group. Watching relevant films and videos, listening to recordings, and examining art and artifacts are all important parts of the research process.

EXCELLENCE

People involved in playbuilding recognize the hard work the process entails. Typically, they gain an understanding of how excellence can occur only with commitment, focus, and a willingness to work through the many stages of the process.

Choosing Topics for Playbuilding

Topics for playbuilding are limitless and can stem from any number of sources in and out of the classroom. Curriculum areas that tend to be good sources of ideas for playbuilding include: science, social studies, language arts, English, family studies, media study, and art.

Playbuilding is an effective way of ensuring that a group engages with ideas, information, and issues on a number of levels. When a group wishes to use playbuilding to explore a topic of immediate concern to them, for example, racism, there will be little debate about the issue and the decision to pursue the play will be relatively harmonious. Conversely, if group members want to playbuild but are unsure of what they want to explore, they may need help in determining a topic. This process should not be rushed; each group member needs time to make a commitment to the topic.

Contexts for Playbuilding

Playbuilding can occur anywhere – in elementary schools or high schools, in community youth groups, or in theatre groups. It is a satisfying way for people of all ages to explore ideas and issues, and to make their views public. It is also an effective way for a group to make a statement about its identity within a community.

Playbuilding is a particularly useful tool within educational institutions. It is, of course, an essential area of exploration within a drama or theatre course. As well, it can help students to make a personal connection with many areas of learning. As an example, a historical event can come alive for students through playbuilding. A geographical region may be physically realized through a playbuilt play that explores its features and cultures.

The physical and cultural context in which a playbuilding project occurs will shape the way the work proceeds, the roles that actors adopt, and the final form of the work.

Ways of Working

There are five essential elements of a playbuilt play:

- a group of actors who agree to work collaboratively,
- agreed-upon ideas or issues,
- a workshop and performance space,
- a director,
- an audience.

Playbuilding can occur with a group of any size. We have playbuilt with groups containing as few as three people and as many as sixty. (This latter group was of nightmarish proportions, but it eventually produced a chronicle play lasting two hours.) We think the ideal group size to be between six and sixteen actors.

Playbuilding can take place in any location. The optimal place is a workshop space that, at least to a minor degree, resembles the performance space. The performance space can be anywhere, but will likely depend on the nature of the play. Among locations where playbuilt plays have been staged are "proper" theatres, school yards, shopping malls, fields, and barns. Some community theatre groups like to take their plays into the community so that the audience can view it in familiar surroundings. As an example, a group working on a play about factory workers performed it on the factory floor. A scout group who developed a play to make a statement to the local community performed its play in a local bush clearing.

Ideas for plays often arise out of the daily lives of the participants. One group of young women developed a playbuilt play called "Female Fallacies" that explored a number of female stereotypes encountered in daily life. Initially, the group members believed that only women were the victims of discrimination. As they explored issues through their playbuilding, they became aware of how males also suffer from similarly constricting stereotypes.

Audiences that attend playbuilt plays are often more specialized or localized than those who attend traditional theatre. The usual playbuilt audience will consist of friends and relatives of the actors, as well as others interested in the issue explored in the play. Playbuilt plays, depending on the topic, may also attract an audience from a regional or special-interest group. In both instances, audience members may not be typical theatre-goers.

Roles in Playbuilding

Whatever the size of the group or the nature of the playbuilding project, there are three main types of roles. In some instances, roles will be allocated to actors or outsiders; at other times, the roles will be more fluid and will be filled by actors on a rotating or short-term basis.

THE CAST

The cast comprises the greatest number of roles, and most cast members are involved in all stages of the play's development.

As well, the cast may be responsible for any furniture, props, or sets needed for the performance.

THE WRITER/DRAMATURGE

Typically, the role of the writer/dramaturge is to record and develop from the workshops the working script for rehearsal. Occasionally, the writer/dramaturge may also be required to produce other material for the group's consideration, or to assist in the researching process.

THE DIRECTOR/DESIGNER

The role of the director is to oversee the planning and leading of workshop sessions and rehearsals. She or he may also be concerned with the final design of the performance, given the group's development of the play. (In a school situation, this role may fall to the teacher, although it can also be assumed by a student.)

Role Assignment

Outlined here are three ways in which roles can be assigned (or not assigned) in a playbuilt play. Descriptions of playbuilding processes in this book have the adult assuming the role of writer/director, the students assuming the role of actors.

1. Writer/director and cast
The roles of writer/dramaturge and director/designer are assumed by one group member while the remainder of the group forms the cast. The writer/director and the cast work together to explore the topic of the play, create the script, and present the group's ideas in dramatic form. The writer/director is responsible for developing the written script and directing the play. She or he is also responsible for planning workshop and rehearsal sessions, and for ensuring that the performances run smoothly.

2. Writer/dramaturge, director/designer, and cast
The writer/dramaturge and director/designer, while having distinct roles and responsibilities, work together with the group to build the play. Together, the writer and director plan the workshop sessions. The director runs the workshops, while the writer records the ideas of the group, writes scenes based on

the workshops, and brings them back to the group for further exploration. The finished script will comprise contributions of all group members, but the final version is the responsibility of the writer. The director's responsibility is to have the group rehearse the script until it is ready for presentation. Any revisions arising from the rehearsal process will be made by the writer.

3. Collaborative creation
No roles are assigned. All group members take part and are responsible for all stages of the playbuilding process. Occasionally, various members will assume the roles of writer/ dramaturge or director/designer on a short-term basis if the group decides this is necessary.

Forms of Playbuilt Plays

Playbuilt plays generally fall into one of two broad categories – narrative or expository.

Narrative Plays

Narrative plays are primarily concerned with telling a story, either one in existence or an original story. When members of a playbuilding group work with an existing story, they will vary one or more aspects, for example, characters' point of view, story context, or story ending. The play may chronicle "true" events in the life of a known or imaginary character, or may retell a particular historical incident.

In the case of an original story, group members may devise its plot through a variety of dramatic explorations or improvisational activities. They may also develop the story from an exploration of a character or characters.

Whether the play is a retelling of an existing story or a presentation of a new story, it will likely comprise a sequence of short episodes. Events are not necessarily presented in chronological order – time sequences may be juxtaposed through the use of dual time sequences, flashbacks, and flashforwards.

Expository Plays

Expository plays are primarily concerned with presenting a viewpoint or arguing a case about an issue. They may include original material, or material derived from other sources. Plays appearing in anthologies are one type of expository play where the form consists of a sequence of scenes based around already existing material, adapted and ordered to make a statement about an issue or theme. An expository play may also be developed through improvisation and workshop activities.

Although expository plays may have a narrative thread running through them, they usually follow a collage or montage format and are structured around a variety of short, thematically linked scenes. Links between scenes are usually established in a similar way to links between differing premises of an argument. Each scene may add something to the previous premise, or it may present an opposing viewpoint.

Sometimes, the collage format will utilize non-naturalistic devices, such as chorus and soundscapes, as a link between and within scenes.

A Comparison of Scripted Plays and Playbuilding

Playbuilding is a collaborative process. It engages the energies and ideas of a group of people in the production of a piece of theatre for performance. While the end product is essentially a piece of theatre, the process of development differs from productions that begin with a ready-made play script that is rehearsed for production.

Scripted Plays

Scripted play productions have recognizable stages of development – the first typically consisting of a director's development of a particular concept for the play. This usually involves considerable research that may include the involvement of a dramaturge and designer. The directorial concept is then translated into plans that form the basis of the rehearsal process.

The rehearsal process generally begins with the casting of acting roles, the first read-through of the script, and the development of scenes and characters in line with the overall directorial concept. The director works with the cast to develop this concept to the point of technical and dress rehearsals. At this time, the director hands over control to the stage manager who handles the final phase of performance before presenting the play to an audience.

While this is a co-operative way of working, there are clearly defined roles, and these roles are held by particular individuals. As an example, the director has ultimate responsibility for concept development and the rehearsal process. The stage manager has responsibility for the production process. The designer is responsible for costumes, set, lighting or sound, while the dramaturge may be responsible for research, revising, adapting, translating, and preparing copy for publicity purposes. The actors are responsible for the presentation of characters and situations to the audience.

All work together to produce the final product. The product, however, is developed from the reference point of the play script. All decisions are made in relation to the script and its realization in a particular theatre space. This is not to suggest that changes are never made to a script – many are refined even at the final rehearsal. If the audience reacts negatively, changes can be made to the script throughout a season.

A final key point concerning scripted plays. Although improvisation is often used by a director and cast during the rehearsal process, its purpose is to explore and uncover layers of the script, rather than to create a script.

Playbuilt Plays

Improvising is central to the playbuilding process and is used to create the performance text. Scripts, which are written toward the end of the process, may contain only rudimentary notation of stage events in the form of a running order and lighting and sound cues.

The playbuilding process relies on a different set of role relationships and on more fluid roles than scripted productions. While one person may be allocated the role of director, for example, other group members may assume this role from time to time throughout the process. In some cases, all members of the group assume responsibility for the directorial concept that emerges through the group's improvisational activities.

Playbuilt plays often fall into the category of non-naturalistic, expository plays. While a playbuilt play may have a narrative through line, chances are that its main focus will be on presenting an argument, arguing a case, and persuading an audience to consider a particular viewpoint. The argument is presented through a series of short thematically linked scenes that developed out of improvisation. Each moment or scene in the playbuilt play presents a stage in the argument and is a premise linked logically, rather than temporally, to those before and after it.

These scenes may focus on one character, a group of characters, or a number of thematically linked characters. Although some scenes may use enactment – action involving characters – they may also use a variety of dramatic techniques including freeze frames, fluid sculptures, slow-motion sculptures, speaking diary, and soliloquy. In addition to realistic dialogue, members of playbuilt plays will often employ other means of communication involving voice, sound, and movement.

2

Principles of playbuilding

Playbuilding and Role Drama

Playbuilding, although a distinctive form of drama/theatre technique, is in some ways related to role drama. Both forms share the following principles:

1. IT IS A GROUP PROCESS.

Role drama and playbuilding are not individual activities. In each case, groups of people must work together to a common end. This group process entails all aspects of establishing relationships and roles for the good of the group. Since roles in both role drama and playbuilding are fluid and flexible, this means juggling roles throughout the process.

2. THE PROCESS IS COLLABORATIVE.

Collaboration means that there is a sharing of power among group members. Decisions are made as part of the group process; all participants have the right to contribute to the decision. Managing this collaboration is a delicate balancing act when working with young people who recognize the decision-making power of adults in society at large.

3. THE PROCESS REQUIRES RIGOROUS THINKING.

Playbuilding and role drama offer participants the chance to engage in a world of ideas and concepts, and to explore ways of representing these ideas through images and metaphor. These activities require creative and critical thinking.

4. THE PROCESS REQUIRES TRUST.

Participants in these drama forms must take risks in trying out ideas and ways of working with the group. This necessitates an atmosphere of trust and support. Developing such an atmosphere is one of the main tasks of the director.

5. THE PROCESS IS AESTHETIC.

Participants of role drama and playbuilding engage in an aesthetic experience. They explore ideas and issues and shape these in terms of the art form of drama and theatre. It is important that the director stress the need for group members to think as artists. Emphasis should be on the work and on making decisions that make the play stronger, rather than on individual egos.

While playbuilding and role drama share these principles, it is important to remember that in at least one area they differ greatly. Role drama does not involve an audience outside of the participants; playbuilding culminates in an outside audience presentation. Although participants in a role drama often serve as an audience for one another, the role drama is not performed to an audience or repeated for different audiences. Consequently, role drama participants do not experience the process of rehearsal.

The action of a role drama happens *now*, in the simple present tense. The action of a playbuilt play occurs in the continuous present. The *now* is repeated for each audience, and each audience shares in the making of the present tense.

The ultimate common goal of playbuilding and role drama is to create and communicate meaning. In role drama, the meaning must be made clear for the participants. In playbuilding, the meaning must be made clear for both the participants and the audience.

The following table shows the similarities and differences between these two approaches to learning through theatre in a school setting.

Playbuilding	Role Drama
Begins with a question: "What topic would you like to explore through a play?" or	Same

Playbuilding	**Role Drama**
Teacher/director presents a topic and gauges whether there is any interest in it. or Director uses some other source as a stimulus, for example, an artifact, song, painting, a costume piece, a letter, or a map. Parts of scripted plays can also be used as a beginning for playbuilding.	Same

All of these sources can be used. Parts of plays or novels can be used, and role drama can help the actors reach new understandings of text. |
Discussion/narrowing of topic: The director asks a number of questions, for example, "What is it that interests you about this topic?" "What do you mean by the topic?" The director and actors choose the focus together.	Director often chooses focus and the key question to be pursued.
Different roles are "tried on" through improvisation and other acting exercises.	Initial roles are selected by director for both actors and director.
A variety of techniques are used to explore the topic. These include those listed for role drama, as well as theatre games, exercises, and acting problems that generate ideas and material. The resulting scenes and images are often recorded.	Building belief and commitment activities are planned by the director, for example, • thinking while director questions • interviewing • drawing • writing • still image • director in role • movement • narration • empty chair
Scenes are repeated, group analyzes, makes suggestions as to how to make meaning clearer or stronger dramatically. Changes are incorporated.	Scenes are *not* repeated. How things appear from the outside is not important. The play must have meaning for the participants.

Playbuilding	Role Drama
Scenes are repeated many times.	
Emphasis is placed on both the internal meaning for the actors and the external meaning for the audience.	
The group discusses and solves acting and playwriting problems. Reflection on the topic is an ongoing process as the topic is explored.	Actors encounter director in role, who presents them with a problem that they tackle in role.
	Reflection is ongoing.
The actors and/or director edits scenes and makes decisions as to what scenes will be in the play. The style and form of the piece are decided.	Further possibilities for the drama develop from the role drama.
	Actors reflect and discuss the issues that have arisen through the drama.
	Often new ideas arise leading to further drama.
The play is often scripted.	The drama is never scripted.
Rehearsals are conducted. The play is polished for an outside group.	The drama is not rehearsed for an audience. Occasionally, aspects are repeated for the group to study and analyze, for example, still image.
The play is performed. Reflection in the form of discussion of the issues in the play with the audience is often a feature of playbuilt plays.	Reflection in the form of talking or writing with the participants is a feature of role drama.

Clearly, playbuilding and role drama share many principles, and at the heart of each is theatre form. However, where role drama springs from theatre, playbuilding takes the actors back into the theatre. This point can best be made by the following diagram.

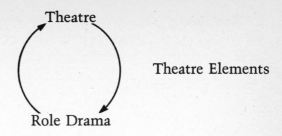

Theatre

Theatre Elements

Role Drama

Starting Playbuilding

People often ask, "How do I start?" There is no one simple
answer to this question since much will depend on you and
your group. If the people with whom you are working are part
of a drama group, they will be comfortable with theatre form
and you can introduce the concept of playbuilding with a
minimum of background information. If you or your group have
little experience with drama, you may want to do some simple theatre games and exercises that will allow actors to get
to know one another and will help to build an atmosphere of
trust. (See bibliography for suggested references.)

A trusting and supportive atmosphere is crucial to the playbuilding process. Encourage actors to support one another's
ideas, and to criticize constructively their own work and that
of others. Actively encourage them to take risks in their exploration of the topic, and stress the need to think as artists to help
keep the play and its creation as the group's central objective.

The playbuilt play begins with an idea and ends with a production. In between, there are definite stages through which
all such plays develop. An understanding of these stages will
enable you and your group to keep in mind the focus of the
process.

Stages in the Playbuilding Process

The playbuilding process may take place over a short period
of time – a day or a week – or it may extend over several
months. It can sometimes appear to be formless and free, with
actors responding to impulses. While these explorations can
and will vary widely, all participants must have some notion

of the forward direction of the work. They need to feel confident that the work is progressing toward the group's ultimate goal of performance. It will be your job to instill this confidence in the cast.

Stages in the process include:

- exploring,
- framing,
- sequencing,
- rehearsing,
- performing.

Exploring

The explorer traverses uncharted territory. Intrepid in her search for new discoveries, she takes risks as she covers unfamiliar ground. Because she is curious and eager to learn everything she can about this new place, the explorer examines everything. She observes using not only her eyes, but all her capacities for sensory perception. She collects samples that will help her to understand what she is discovering, and uses all available sources of information. Ultimately, the explorer begins to sift through what she has found, recording and discussing the implications of these observations in order to construct a pattern in her discoveries.

The initial stage of playbuilding is also an exploration of unknown territory. This stage has three important components:

- Dramatic exploration of the topic
- Researching
- Assimilating observations

While these aspects need not be seen as separate entities, they can be seen as forming a sequence.

1. DRAMATIC EXPLORATION OF THE TOPIC.

Members of the group discuss their knowledge of and feelings about the topic to be explored. This discussion helps to establish a common shared understanding that encourages dramatic exploration, which involves the use of drama techniques as a means of exploring issues.

Many playbuilding groups flounder before they begin because they start their exploration of a topic with a brainstorming session. While this is one way to begin, and many groups do begin here, there are dangers in using brainstorming as a sole starting strategy.

The first danger centres on the fact that verbal language is an effective tool in constructing power relations. Brainstorming, as a verbal process, can give rise to the establishment of a network of power relations that may not necessarily lead to the best dramatic results. Those group members who are most dominant and verbal can, through brainstorming, assert their control and direction of the exploration from the start.

The second danger concerns the limits that may be put on defining the topic by exploring it only through verbal language. As a result, dramatic possibilities of some ideas may not be explored simply because they do not lend themselves to verbal dialogue. Drama should and does use much more than linguistic codes of communication. It relies on visual and sound codes, as well as on specific codes that have to do with performing in a particular space and with particular technical effects.

The use of all modes of communication needs to inform the early explorations of a playbuilding activity. Initial dramatic explorations should encourage participants to think in all codes – linguistic, visual, sound, and movement. This entails the use of techniques such as depictions/tableaux/still pictures, freeze frames, sculpting images, soundscapes, sound collages, fluid sculptures, movement, dumbshow, or mime. The group may engage in these activities as a whole group or by breaking into smaller groups.

An important tactic to use at this stage of exploration involves limiting the use of language though silent negotiation. When this tactic is applied, the group cannot talk, signal, point, or gesture during the creation of a depiction. The following example illustrates the process of silent negotiation.

A group chooses the topic of holidays to explore through playbuilding. The director gives these directions:

"Form small groups of four or five members. In each group, one person come forward and begin a still image that says something about holidays. The rest of the group will observe this member carefully, try to interpret what she or he is saying, and add to that idea by joining the still image.

> "Take your time and be thoughtful. Make sure that you are adding to the meaning of what is being portrayed. This process will be complete when all group members are a part of the still image."

Silent negotiation is one of the most effective techniques to ensure that the focus remains on dramatic aspects and group collaboration.

Here is another example of silent negotiation. In this instance, nine actors, aged fifteen to sixteen, have selected the topic of dreams for playbuilding.

> With no discussion of the topic, the actors begin to create an unorchestrated soundscape that expresses their initial thoughts on dreams. They use a tape recorder and work on the soundscape until it comes to a natural close. The actors then listen to the recording and, without further discussion, create a movement piece in response to the soundscape. This activity, like the creation of the soundscape, is not orchestrated.
>
> The actors then discuss briefly their responses and decide to explore two moments in the soundscape they feel are particularly strong. One moment is hypnotic and softly sensual, the second is strident and nightmarish. The actors divide themselves into two groups, one of which will explore the hypnotic moment, the other the strident moment.
>
> Each group uses silent negotiation to create a depiction of the moment. The groups then observe the other's work. The director asks the remaining class members to respond to each depiction by creating captions or thought/speech balloons for the characters.
>
> With little discussion, the groups decide to explore these speech balloons as first line/last line improvisations. After they have explored a number of improvisational outcomes, the groups join the rest of the class to discuss what they have discovered.

In this example, the group began its explorations using a dramatic mode, which was followed by discussion and reflection. Group members discovered that the ideas which surfaced from the group work were very different from their initial, individual thoughts.

This improvisation comprised only the topic and the actors – there was no script and no director. The group established a collaborative pattern of working at the outset, negating the need for assigned roles.

An outcome of this initial exploration was a series of questions that arose from the work and which led the group automatically to the next stage of exploration – researching. Does everyone dream? Do animals dream? How do you interpret dreams? The answers to these questions would be found in a variety of ways, from researching science books through talking with people about their dreams.

2. RESEARCHING.

Research undertaken for playbuilding must be broad-based in order for the answers to stimulate further dramatic exploration. For example, finding only one source to answer a question will provide insufficient information on which to base further work. Ideally, information will be researched in an academic mode (e.g., finding answers to questions in books, periodicals, and other source material). These answers will then be combined with the stories, conversations, pictures, and images that are part of our contemporary life. The documenting of research findings should be as broad-based as the research process. Written records, pictorial records, and sound recordings are codes essential to drama.

Sharing research findings helps actors to place initial explorations in a wider context. They need to understand, however, that while they may have amassed a great deal of material, not all of it will or need be used to inform further explorations.

"Our group decided to pursue several sources of research. We identified questions that were factual in nature, such as do animals dream, questions that required people to tell us personal experiences, such as the most terrible dream they have had, and questions that would require direct observation, such as how people react to dreams when they are sleeping.

"Our group divided into teams so we could explore these questions. Some of us did library research, returning with written material. Some of us talked with people, recording their stories on tape. Others took photographs of people sleeping in some unusual places like homeless people sleeping on park benches.

> Finally, some of us watched children as they slept and took photographs of them in their beds. This research helped us to build on our moment from the soundscape."

3. ASSIMILATING OBSERVATIONS.

The photographs helped to focus further work for this group. In one photograph, a dog lay beside a person sleeping on a park bench. In another, a sleeping child clutched a fluffy toy dog. These contrasting images, viewed in light of earlier explorations and the focus question about whether animals dream, redirected the group's thinking about the topic they had chosen.

The dramatic exploration/discussion/research/discussion cycle may propel the group into the next phase of the playbuilding process.

Framing

The second stage of the process focuses on the construction of the play's framework. Groups have generated material through dramatic exploration and research, and are now ready to develop the play's performance possibilities.

A single idea may be expressed in a number of ways in performance. The main consideration, at this stage, is to find the best way to dramatically express the ideas of the group. It is important for playbuilding participants to explore beyond dialogue, and to take into account dramatic devices such as on-stage audience, chorus, soliloquy, and other devices that allow meaning to be communicated to an audience.

In the process of framing the play, the group needs to consider how the elements of drama can be manipulated in order to clarify meaning. To do this, group members need to examine the use of focus, tension, contrast, symbol, rhythm, and mood to ensure that the meaning is clearly articulated.

In tightening the frame, the group needs to return to their initial explorations or scenes and rework them so that they are dramatically effective. This part of the process is akin to the drafting process in writing, where the initial expression of an idea is rewritten to make the communication clearer for the reader.

An important part of this process involves actors stepping in and out of the work in order to watch it from the point of view of the audience and to provide feedback to the cast. All actors need to know what they are communicating to their audience before the work is finalized. Often, there is a discrepancy between what actors think they are communicating and the message the audience receives. On occasion, an audience's feedback can influence how the group alters the play's development or message.

Techniques that assist in this process include freezing moments, having the audience caption frames and hot-seat characters with questioning, increasing tension by reducing the time in which an action can happen, and playing a scene in slow motion or fast forward.

The group now reworks their explorations. The photograph of the person on the bench provides the stimulus for further explorations that include a monologue followed by a hot seating; a somnambulist movement piece explored through slow motion and fast forward; and a dual action piece that examines dreams as a form of escape, done in a series of freeze frames.

Group members decide that the dual action piece makes a strong statement about how dreams allow people to escape the reality of the present and live for a moment in a fantasy world. The tightening of this frame reminds the group of the T.S. Eliot poem, "Rhapsody on a Windy Night," which suggests that dreams bring back all of a person's monsters in one swirling moment throughout the night. The group's exploration of this poem provides the dramatic framing which originated from the two opposite views first identified in the soundscape. The ticking of a clock cited in Eliot's poem brings the actors back to their first soundscape. They use some of the sounds they recorded earlier to express the concept of time passing as a person dreams. This image of time further cements the contours of the frame and shows a possible overall structure.

The general shape of the play develops as the process of dramatic framing continues. This leads into the next stage of the play's development.

Sequencing

Stories in playbuilt plays can be recounted in chronological order, or through the use of a variety of flashback or flashforward techniques. These plays typically have an episodic structure that may toy with or disregard chronological time sequences when actors are intent on juxtaposing contrasting moments.

The sequencing of dramatic moments must be considered when selecting material for the play since it can have a tremendous effect on the message conveyed to the audience. When the sequence is altered, audiences can sometimes view the same material but receive a very different view of the topic.

One way to begin this stage is to consider the statement each moment will make to the audience. Start by listing all moments. Consider what line of argument might be constructed by varying the sequence of these moments. This will help actors to consider the meaning made by juxtaposing two scenes.

Sequencing involves selecting and eliminating moments. Some moments that have been an essential part of the exploration and framing process may need to be discarded while new material may need to be developed. While a group member may be loath to eliminate his or her favorite moment, it is important for all actors to realize that some moments may not have a place in the final structure of the play. Perhaps the best test is to ask what statement the moment makes, and then determine how that statement fits in with the play's message. If the moment doesn't connect logically with the rest of the work, it must be discarded.

The process of sequencing also involves an examination of the ways in which moments, episodes, and scenes are linked. There are a number of ways this may be done, including the use of music, blackouts, and narration. It is important to consider how the linking device will act as a comment upon the adjacent scenes.

The group now has a number of possible episodes, each of which makes some statement about dreams and the process of dreaming. From the various scenes and episodes they have explored, the actors select seven episodes that make the following statements:

Everyone dreams, including animals.
Dreams let us imagine ourselves in other situations.
Dreams let us pretend to be other people.
In dreams, we perform heroic deeds.
In dreams, we do things we would not do in real life.
Dreams place us in terrifying situations.
Whatever our dreams, we return to the same real world in the morning.

The group's selection of episodes is made largely on the basis of the coherence of the overall statement. Actors discard scenes that explore the notion of dreams recapturing past experiences, primarily because they want to keep the focus on the idea of returning to the present from an imagined future. They discard other scenes that explore aspects of wish fulfillment and nightmares in order to keep the piece building to the single nightmarish climax of the last dream sequence and the reality of the day.

The process of sequencing also requires that the group consider production aspects, particularly those that might need to be developed, acquired, or built. It is at this point that design decisions need to be made. As the performance time approaches, all production elements – script, sound, lights, costumes, props, and scenery – must work together as a total piece of theatre.
   Production and design decisions that must be made include:

- Venue. The space where the play will be performed will influence the set and lighting. It will also influence entrances, exits, and the shape of the playing area.
- Set. Is this to be an elaborate or simple affair?
- Costumes. If actors are to wear costumes, do they serve the play by adding to its mood and message? Are masks to be used? Will there be costume changes? If yes, can the venue meet this need?
- Props. Are props necessary, or are they included as an extra frill? The following rules will help you determine the necessity of a prop:

1. Discard a prop if it doesn't add to the play.
2. Keep your stage and design simple.
3. Remove unneeded props from a set.

4. Ensure that costumes, sets, and props add to the overall statement you are making with the play. Avoid unnecessary backdrops.

As the director, you will now need to make notes concerning the form of the play. Try to keep these notes to a minimum. Include the running order of scenes (indicate entrances and exits), and sound, lighting, and stage changes.

Running Order

Dreams: Whole-group chorus
Other Places: Live dog/movement piece/music/props – dog basket, collar, rug, lead
Other People: Fluffy dog – monologue/mask
Great Achievements: Woman/mime/freeze/dissolve/V/O/ soundscape
Escaping the Reality: Woman/duologues
Beware Your Dreams: "Rhapsody on a Windy Night" – poem/voice movement – whole group
The Last Twist of the Knife: Whole-group chorus

Rehearsing

The time spent rehearsing a playbuilt play is usually much shorter than that spent rehearsing a scripted production. This is due, in large part, to the amount of exploratory work done in the process of developing the play. The bulk of rehearsal time should be spent on scene changes, links between scenes, and the rhythm and pace of the scenes in relation to one another. Time spent on scene changes is crucial, especially if the play has a large cast and/or the changes are made with lights on, in front of the audience, rather than in a blackout.

Performing

This is the moment that everyone has been working toward! Whether the audience is another class that will view the play in a classroom or a public audience that will view the play in a theatre, the presentation of the work is the culmination of the process and is an exciting time for the actors.

At the end of the play, actors can introduce themselves to the audience and, if appropriate, answer any questions. On occasion, audiences will not have been exposed to a play where the focus is on exploring an issue through non-naturalistic theatre techniques. In this case, you may choose to have the actors field questions about the process of creating the play. Rehearse this question-and-answer period so that actors are comfortable interacting with the audience. The ensuing dialogue between cast and audience members can be a valuable learning experience for everyone, and clearly illustrates the learning potential of playbuilding.

3

Creating a play in a day –
a simple formula for playbuilding

It is possible to create a simple playbuilt play in as little as three or four hours. The following description is of one such play, created with a group of twenty secondary school students, aged twelve to sixteen. Five of the students had taken part in school dramas, the remaining fifteen were drama novices. The students, who were volunteers for the project, formed a demonstration group for a professional development day. The playbuilding session took place over a period of four hours, however, it would be possible to use this format to playbuild a play in four one-hour sessions or eight half-hour sessions.

Session One: Introducing Playbuilding and Establishing the Rules

The director explains the process of playbuilding to the group. She tells the actors that they are going to create a play in four hours and then perform the play for a small, invited audience. She outlines how playbuilt plays differ from standard drama pieces in that they do not tell a story in the standard sense. Instead, playbuilt plays explore actors' thoughts and emotions on a certain topic. This is a difficult concept for the group to understand, but actors tell the director they will trust her on this issue.

Playbuilt plays are, in essence, collages built around a central theme. People who have not experienced this type of play often think in terms of creating a linear story, rather than a series of thematically linked images. Further, the concept of theatre held by many young people is colored by television and half-hour sitcoms. Building an atmosphere where the group trusts that the director knows what she or he is doing is vital when working at this pace.

She mentions these elements as crucial to the group's success:

- Based on their interests, actors choose the topic of play. A director's interest in the topic is incidental: his or her role is to work with the actors to help them shape their ideas into dramatic form.
- They should avoid using television shows or movies as a topic. The point of a playbuilt play is to create an original piece of theatre.
- The topic should be of sufficient interest to all actors, and one that they would like to devote four hours to exploring.
- Given the time limit, it is helpful if actors choose a topic on which they are knowledgeable.

Young people often want to tackle subjects on which they have little knowledge. This is a good strategy if the group has time to research the topic – building a play can be a powerful force to motivate actors to gain the necessary knowledge. When time constraints are imposed on a project, however, research is not possible.

In a situation where you have to present a play for a particular occasion, for example, Remembrance Day, raise the issue of developing a play on this topic with the actors. If their reaction is mixed, it is best to drop the subject and let them playbuild on another day where there is no topic restriction.

The director asks the actors if they can:

- work quickly,
- co-operate,
- listen carefully to one another's ideas,
- be ready to have fun and to work hard.

They agree that they can meet these criteria.

Choosing the Topic

The director asks that the actors brainstorm ideas for topics, keeping an open mind and not reacting to the topics as they are offered. All topics will be accepted and recorded on the board. As well, actors are reminded to choose topics that interest them and which they know something about.

The group begins to offer topics, hesitantly at first, but soon the board is filled with suggestions, including: relationships, school, opportunities, comedy, suicide, sports, doors, images, rape, violence, AIDS, music, soccer, gum, death, divorce, friends, enemies, fears, and families. All topics are accepted without comment by the director who also makes it clear that she will not accept members of the group reacting to another person's topics by laughing, moaning, or being derisive in any way.

The seriousness of subjects raised, even by younger people, is often surprising. As evidence of this fact, a recent list of playbuilding topics generated by a group of eleven- and twelve-year-olds included violence, AIDS, and child abuse. Drama offers young people a safe way to explore such issues. There will always be topics, however, with which you may not be prepared to deal. In this instance, tell the group how you feel: you are a partner in this endeavor so your opinion counts, too. Saying something like, "I feel that I wouldn't want to take on the responsibility of helping to create a play on suicide. It is too sensitive a subject for me and is too big a responsibility" is usually sufficient. That said, we have found that we usually do not have to censor topics as actors will usually veer away from those that will be too difficult for them, or too upsetting for an audience.

Narrowing the Topic

The director asks the group if there is at least one topic on the board that interests each of them. The group affirms this. She then tells them that, since they must work quickly, they will have only three chances to vote for a topic. Students have a few minutes to review the topics listed on the board before voting begins. Topics that receive no votes are erased. Eight topics remain after the first vote: families, relationships, soccer, sports, doors, violence, gum, and friends.

The amount of votes allowed the group depends on the time available. If you have more than four hours, give the group the opportunity to hold additional votes.

The director requests that someone who voted for the first topic, "families," stand up and try to sell this idea to the group. A boy volunteers and attempts to promote the idea of "families" as a topic by giving some of his ideas for the play. This process is repeated for each of the remaining seven topics. A lively few minutes ensues as volunteers try various techniques to sway the group to their topic.

Actors must now vote on the eight topics. After the vote, three topics are left: violence, relationships, and sports. The director asks the group if these topics can be combined and if there is a relationship between them. A group discussion on how violence occurs in both sports and relationships follows. The actors who want to work with the topic of relationships, however, do not want to combine these ideas, and insist this was not want they wanted when they voted for relationships.

At this stage, it is important that you do not impose your ideas on the group. Young people are often quick to discern what you want and, in an effort to please, will agree to that topic. If this happens, they will look constantly to you for guidance. Asking questions often helps them to clarify ideas. "What is it that interests you about this topic?" "How do you see these two ideas working together?" "If we did do our play on sports, is there any way we could incorporate relationships?" This type of discussion, although time consuming, is invaluable as it crystallizes the actors' ideas and helps them to make a decision.

After the director asks the group to vote for one of these topics, only relationships and violence remain. As the first hour ends, the director asks if the group can agree on violence as a topic since it received the most votes. The group that opted for relationships is not happy – they want the play to explore their topic. The director asks the actors if they would be willing to try to incorporate some of their ideas under the heading of violence so work could begin. They agree reluctantly.

If the topic has not been agreed to by all members, the project is doomed. Sometimes, two opposing groups in the class will not compromise. In this instance, you can either do two plays at once (hard to do since it involves working through all steps with two topics and two groups), or you can choose the topic with the most votes and promise to do the other topic at a later date.

Session Two: Still Image

The director suggests that the actors work in groups of two, three, or five members to create a still image that says something about violence. She also explains that they will use the technique of silent negotiation to create this image. A volunteer from each group steps forward and freezes in a stance that suggests violence. The rest of the group silently "reads" the image and then, one at a time, joins the actor and adds to the image. Each group's image is negotiated silently. In a short time, there are four powerful images that make a statement about the topic.

Silent negotiation enables the group to work together in a non-verbal and co-operative fashion. The image will not work unless each member can read and respond to his or her peer's message. This method of communicating produces results much faster than discussion. As well, actors may not have an idea of what their stance looks like until it is read silently by peers.

Showing and Reading Images

The director tells the actors to relax, but to try to remember where they were in the image. Each group will now show their image to the others. As members assemble for the other groups, the director asks them to mimic their original stance as closely as possible since even small changes will alter the image. She also stresses that they must not tell the meaning of their image. The other actors, as readers, will make suggestions that will often be nowhere near the messages the group members are trying to show. This is fine since the point of the activity is not to guess correctly, but to generate as many ideas as possible. The director asks questions, for example, "Who are these people?" "What is going on here?" "Where are they?" "What is their relationship to each other?" "What do you think this group is saying about violence?" "If this were a picture in the paper, what would the caption be?" The readers give a variety of responses.

Asking the right questions is at the heart of good teaching. Much has been written about questioning as a teaching technique. For more information on questioning, see the bibliography.

The group is praised for holding the image. It is now the next group's turn. As well as the questions asked of the first group, the director indicates one of the characters in the still image and asks, "What is this woman thinking?" "If she were a character in a book, what would she say?" She indicates others in the still image, asking "What might this character be saying?" "Is there dialogue here? What would it be?"

At this stage, group members are being asked to think in dialogue, like a playwright. Previously, they used language to describe and speculate.

After the last group has created its still image, the director tells its members that she would like them to bring this image to life. At the count of three, group members spring to life and use dialogue to illustrate their relationships. When the director says "Freeze" after a period of twenty seconds, the actors stop. The groups observing these actors briefly discuss what they have seen.

Here this inexperienced group is being edged into improvisation in a painless way. They have only a few minutes to think while the director explains about bringing their image to life. The improvisation lasts for twenty seconds, giving the audience sufficient time to observe the group. At the end of the improvisation, audience members share their observations with the group.

The director tells all groups to bring their image to life. They can use their initial idea, one suggested through audience observation, or a new idea. The one rule at this point is that they must begin and end in a scene. This requires that group members know who they are, where they are, and what's going on between them.

Until this stage, the group has worked as writers through generating ideas. They are now about to move into performance and work like actors. Freezing the improvisation at the beginning and end makes each group's message clearer to the audience while providing actors with a beginning and end point.

The four groups work on their improvisations. The director circulates and gives a few suggestions, mostly about blocking. The four scenes are:

1. a fight starts in a school playground by some bullies,
2. a drunken father comes home and terrorizes his family,
3. a couple has a heated and violent argument over the young woman wanting to dissolve the relationship, and
4. players have a "punch up" in ice hockey.

Each group shows their scene. The director asks if anyone can make suggestions that would enable the actors to better communicate their scene to the audience. As one example, audience members found the fight scene in the hockey game confusing so the director suggests they try it again in slow motion. The group repeats the scene and it meets with greater success. Suggestions about blocking are made, and some details are changed. The director asks everyone to help give a name to each scene. They become, in order, "The Bullies," "No, Dad!" "The Break-Up," and "Fight!"

The director explains to the actors that they would create more scenes for the play if they had more time. These additional scenes would provide each group with a selection to choose from for their final performance. However, as they are working to a tight time schedule, each group will work with the scenes they have come up with to this point. She gives them ten minutes to rehearse their scenes. While the groups are engaged with rehearsal, the director creates a sheet of "one liners."

Session Three: Creating and Rehearsing One Liners

"One liners" are open-ended sentences on a topic that are intended to generate ideas and lines for the play. The director prepares the following sheet of one liners and gives a copy to each actor.

Violence is . . . .
When I think of violence, I . . . .
People who are in violent relationships . . . .

In our family, violence . . . .
When I see violent films, I . . . .
When it comes to violence, I . . . .

The director calls the group together and explains the purpose of the one-liner sheets. The lines they generate through the use of this page may be used to begin and end the play. She asks the actors to finish each sentence with the first thought that comes into their head. She tells them that the sheets are anonymous so they do not have to censor their thoughts. No discussion is allowed as they complete the lines. As soon as each person finishes, she or he gives the sheet to the director and sits with her in another part of the room. When more than five people have handed in their sheets, the director gives them to the group of actors who are sitting with her. They read each sheet before exchanging them with one another. Soon, all the actors have finished writing and the majority have read the pages. The director then collects the pages and gives one to each actor. She discourages them from trying to identify the author of the page. Each actor reads his or her page silently, and selects one line that she or he would like to read in the play. Sitting on the floor, each actor reads his or her line aloud. Here are some of the lines that are read aloud:

- When I think of violence, I think I'll be hurt.
- In our family, violence is part of the way we live.
- In our family, violence is something we are all afraid of.
- Violence is all around us.
- When I see violent films, I get excited. I think they are usually funny.
- When it comes to violence, I run.

Rehearsing One Liners

The director marks out one end of the room that will serve as the stage. She asks the actors to arrange themselves in this space so that they will face the audience. She also arranges levels in this area by using some desks at the back of the stage, and four chairs that will be used in some scenes. The room looks like this:

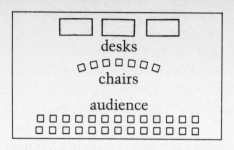

The actors are told to sit, stand, lie or kneel in this space, using the chairs and desks at the back as well as the space on the floor. The group arranges themselves, and the stage picture is quite pleasing. Two people, however, have to move since they block other actors. When the director has checked the stage from various parts of the room, she is assured that the audience will be able to see all of them.

It is now time for the actors to rehearse their one liners. They begin in a frozen position and most move to another frozen position before, during, or after saying their line. The director demonstrates, using the line, "When I think of violence, I think of hockey" from one of the pages. First sitting on a chair, she stands, says her line, and then sits in a different position. She urges the actors to keep it simple, but to express what the line says and to try several ways to express it. They rehearse their line at least ten times, committing the line to memory.

This group rehearsal is a good way for inexperienced actors to gain confidence. It is noisy, as all actors work at the same time. It is often necessary to urge the group to be noisier, to project their voices more, and to have fun while experimenting with how the line will be said. Because the actors are on stage in front of the director, it is easy to see who is having trouble and needs help. For many actors new to playbuilding, this is not an easy task. While it sounds simple, inexperienced actors will need plenty of rehearsing and encouraging at this point.

The director assigns each member of the group a number and has them number off. She asks that they note who came before and after them as this is the order in which the one liners will be presented. The group then presents the one liners.

After listening to the one liners, you may decide to rearrange them but be warned that this process takes time. Building this part of the play is rather like designing an overture. You might make choices based on voice (some lighter, some heavier), make a point by juxtaposing two opposing points of view, or follow a poignant statement with an amusing statement. It's surprising how many times the random order is often the best order for the lines.

The director works with actors who are having difficulty projecting their voices. She stands at the back of the room and urges them to think about her as an audience member. She notes that one of the lines, "In our family, violence is part of the way we live" would be a perfect introduction to the scene, "No, Dad." As a consequence, she moves the actor to the end so that his line will be followed by that scene. The lines are rehearsed again. The director suggests that the groups react to each line with either a sound, word, or gesture. The beginning "one-liner script" now looks like this:

Draft Script – Violence

Actors are sitting, standing on stage in various attitudes. They are frozen, and only come out of their freeze to either give lines, or react to an actor delivering lines.

ACTOR 1: When I think of violence, I think I will be hurt.
GROUP: (Move in one second to a cowering position, with a sound that is like air being punched out of them. FREEZE.)
ACTOR 2: Violence is all around us.
GROUP: (Take up tough attitudes, say Yeah! FREEZE.)
ACTOR 4: When I see violent films, I get excited. I think they are usually funny.
GROUP: (Laugh and point as if to a screen. FREEZE.)
ACTOR 5: I get scared.
GROUP: (Clap hands and say BOO! FREEZE)

The ideas for the group reactions came from both the director and the actors. In the rehearsal, the director asks the actors to react spontaneously to the one liners. She then observes actions the actors make. When she sees one that she thinks is very good, she asks the actor to show everyone, saying, "I think that looks great. Shall we all do that? Let's give it a go."

If there is no reaction, she may have to make suggestions or ask the group to think about it for a minute. Young actors come up with great ideas – you must observe carefully and help them incorporate ideas.

The director has the actors think about the order of the scenes. Given that they will go from one liners to "No, Dad," she wants them to determine the rest of the performance order. Actors discuss this issue and come up with the following order:

One Liners
No Dad
Bullies
Fight
The Break-Up

Each group tells the director their last line and she records them. These lines are needed in order to cue for music, which will be the responsibility of the director. It is important that the cue lines remain constant, as they will be used by both the director and the actors. The director stresses this fact with the actors.

Session Four: Developing a Beginning and an Ending, and Rehearsing the Play

The director questions the actors on stage set-up. "How will we all get on stage? Remember that we are working with lights at all times so we have to make the changes smoothly." The actors suggest coming on in lines, running on as if they were in a playground, or walking on stage in a random fashion with music playing. These ideas are viable, but the director and group agree that the entrance needs to build the mood of the play. After some discussion, the group agrees that actors will come on in pairs, as though they were having a discussion. They would split from their partners into frozen positions that suggest they have walked away from a potential argument. This sparks an idea from one of the actors for the final part of the play – everyone on stage takes part in a violent argument and then a freeze. The director tells the student she will think about the idea, and they can explore it later.

The entire group rehearses coming in and then freezing for the one liners. The director then has all actors move to the last one liner to practise setting up for the first scene. On the cue, "In our family, violence is part of the way we live," the four actors who are in the scene move the chairs into place while members of the other groups sit on the side. The director takes the group through the changes for each scene so the actors can practise where they will be sitting when not in a scene. They also practise moving the furniture.

This kind of rehearsal is called "cue to cue." Rehearsing moves between scenes so that they are smooth and organized will determine a sloppy or polished performance. Actors need practice in thinking through where they are needed. The technician, in this instance the director, needs to practise cueing the music.

When the group finishes the last scene, "The Break Up," one of the actors reminds the director about the suggestion concerning the final part of the play. The groups agree that the idea is good so they decide to rehearse the scene. With all groups on stage, the noise is deafening and violent. A problem occurs when the groups are to freeze – the din drowns out the cue. One actor suggests that her scream could act as the cue. The group tries this alternative. The scream is electrifying, and all actors instinctively turn toward her. The director calls "Freeze." It's a great ending. The four-hour playbuilding session ends with a fifteen-minute rehearsal before the small audience of friends and family arrive!

The Script – Violence

LIGHTS OUT.
LIGHTS ON. (In this case, classroom lights.)
MUSIC.

Two actors come on stage. They are arguing about who is to blame for some gossip at school (improvised). Other pairs enter arguing about other issues (improvised). The level of argument is fairly subdued. When all actors are on stage, each pair parts in exasperation and takes up a frozen attitude.

MUSIC, WHICH HAS BEEN PLAYING IN BACKGROUND, STOPS WHEN
ACTORS FREEZE.

ACTOR 1: When I think of violence, I think I will be hurt.
   GROUP: (Take up attitudes of cowering, with a sound that is
          like air being punched out of them. FREEZE)
ACTOR 2: Violence is all around us.
   GROUP: (Take up tough attitudes, say Yeah! FREEZE.)
ACTOR 4: When I see violent films, I get excited. I think they
          are usually funny.
   GROUP: (Laugh and point as if to a screen. FREEZE.)
ACTOR 5: I get scared.
   GROUP: (Clap hands and say BOO! FREEZE.)

(ONE LINERS CONTINUE UNTIL LAST ACTOR – #20)

ACTOR 20: In our family, violence is part of the way we live.
MUSIC UP. GROUP MOVES CHAIRS FOR "NO DAD!" SCENE. REST OF
ACTORS RETIRE TO THE SIDES WHERE THEY SIT AND WATCH SCENE.
WHEN THE GROUP HAS MOVED CHAIRS AND ACTORS ARE IN PLACE
IN A FROZEN POSITION, MUSIC FADES.

Scene: "No Dad!" The scene is set at the dinner table. A drunken
father abuses his wife while the children try to calm him. The
climax of the scene comes as he is about to hit the mother. One
of the children jumps up, grabs his arm, and yells "No, Dad!"
FREEZE. MUSIC. Chairs are placed at the back of the stage as the
cast of "The Bullies" comes on stage.

Scene: "The Bullies." In this scene, a group of younger kids are
terrorized by bullies who take their lunch money and threaten
to rough them up or beat them. The scene ends with one of the
bullies saying, "Now, get lost kid."
FREEZE. MUSIC. The actors from this scene retire, and the actors
for "Fight" take their place.

Scene: "Fight." This scene is a straight movement piece in slow
motion, and ends when one boy lies injured on the ice. The boy
who hit him looks at him and is horrified.
FREEZE. MUSIC. The actors for the scene "The Break-Up" take
their places while the "Fight" actors leave the stage.

Scene: "The Break-Up." This scene ends with the young man about to hit the young woman. "Don't forget who is boss!" he says.

FREEZE. MUSIC. "The Break-Up" characters leave the stage.

A pair of actors enter arguing about the last scene. They have opposing views about what the young woman should do. They stand centre, continuing their argument as other pairs enter and become involved in the same argument. The argument becomes loud and violent. A young woman on the outskirts of the crowd screams. The group turns to her and freezes.

LIGHTS OUT.

MUSIC. Actors take their bows.

Some Important Tips

If you lack time, have the group do a few "cue to cue" runs, rather than rehearsing the entire play. Because scenes are improvised, it won't matter if they differ each time. The actors, however, must give the right cues or music cues will not be correct. Also, the smooth movements of the actors and the shifting of furniture give polish to a play. All actors should know where they are going *all* the time, and should understand that moving furniture and moving themselves into place is an important part of the play. Train your actors to move efficiently and purposefully from one place to the next – it will impress the audience and make your actors feel professional. Watching actors transform themselves from characters in the play to stagehands is always interesting for the audience, provided the changes are rehearsed and fluid. Don't "black out" between scenes; instead, let the audience see your actors working as stage hands. It is more interesting than blackness and the sound of things moving in the dark.

Having the whole cast on stage during the entire performance eliminates problems of backstage noise and missed cues. Also, the group watching on stage remains a part of the performance. Their faces and bodies reflect the mood of the play, thus making them an interesting part of the action.

If you follow these steps, we think that you will be able to create a theatre piece that is satisfying for actors to create and interesting for audiences to watch. Although there are hundreds of other ways to create a play – some of them are described in this book – this method works and provides you with a basic formula for playbuilding. You can also use this structure when you and your actors have more time to work since it provides a sound starting point.

A word about one liners. They can be used after the topic has been chosen to generate ideas. Scenes can then be built from the ideas stemming from the one liners. As well, they can be used as a device for completing the play and for setting up between scenes. One liners are a useful device that often provides a summary of the group's thinking on the topic.

A Summary of Quick Playbuilding

1. Group determines a topic:
   - brainstorm,
   - vote on two topics,
   - actors "sell" their ideas to the group,
   - have a final vote.
2. In groups, actors create still images that express their ideas on the topic. Remember who, where, and what.
3. Each group shows a still image while the rest of the group "reads" it and gives it a name.
4. Still images are brought to life.
5. Other groups make suggestions to improve the scenes.
6. One liners are completed by the entire group.
7. One-liner sheets are handed out. Each actor chooses his or her line to say in the play.
8. Rehearse one liners.
9. Decide on a beginning and an end.
10. Rehearse scenes.
11. Choose a way to link the scenes.
12. Script the play.
13. Rehearse.
14. Perform.

A Note about Linking and Music

Recorded music, although the simplest way to link scenes, is not the only way. Other devices that can be used include:

chants, soundscape, "Greek chorus," movement, dance, song, jokes, patter by a Master of Ceremonies and one liners. The ideal method to link scenes is to employ a live musician with a synthesizer who can create sound effects and music. She or he can also underscore scenes, creating mood and atmosphere.

If you use recorded music, group members can often be the best source of help. Ask them to identify what they believe to be suitable music for the piece. If possible, they can bring in tapes or CDs so that the rest of the group can listen to their selections. Collectively, the group then decides what music will be included.

You may also bring in music that you think supports the drama. Be prepared, however, for rejection. I once offered Carole King's, "You've Got a Friend" to a group who was creating a play on friendship. I thought it was perfect. Actors listened politely and then said "It's very old." Needless to say they chose something more contemporary.

4

Songs, Shakespeare, and other forms of inspiration

A number of sources can be used as a springboard into playbuilding, including songs, photos, paintings, slides, speeches, poems, letters, magic boxes, maps, and novels. The possibilities are endless.

In this chapter, we describe playbuilding sessions that spring from sources or techniques not cited elsewhere in this book.

Scenes Created from Songs

The following pages outline a session involving a group of fourteen actors, most of whom were between the ages of fourteen and sixteen. The playbuilding project was based on the exploration of songs. This session looks at the group's work with one song, "Who Am I?"

The creation of the play required the actors to be reflective. Anxious that this might make some actors feel vulnerable, the director avoided anything that hinted at "psycho drama." She decided that the actors could create characters for the play who bore no resemblance to themselves. She reasoned that while they would use a part of themselves to create a character, they would be protected, to a degree, by the act of developing fictitious characters.

The following session was conducted during the first week of the project.

1. INTRODUCING THE SONG

With the musical director, the group learns the words to the song, "Who Am I?"

Who Am I?

Who am I?
Who are you?
Everything I say, you say too.
Every move I make,
Every breath I take,
Oh for goodness sake,
Who are you?

2. DISCUSSION

The director asks the group, "What does this song suggest to you?" which leads to a discussion of the song's themes. The director writes the topic – who am I? – on the board and records the group's responses to the song. Sample responses include:

- someone who is talking to himself because there is no one else to talk to,
- someone who is asking, "Why was I born?" and wishing they hadn't been,
- a misfit writing about not fitting in,
- a person who is frightened to grow up because she won't meet her parents' expectations,
- a kid sitting and thinking in a school hallway,
- someone who doesn't know who he is or what's going on.

3. DRAMA EXERCISE

The director presents the group with a variety of pictures cut from magazines and books. Pictures, which are mounted on sheets of cardboard, are spread around the room. (Those in the pictures and those in the class appear to be the same age.) The actors walk around and look at each of the pictures.

The director asks the actors to look at all pictures carefully. She tells each actor to pick one picture that she or he feels attracted to or finds interesting. When the actors have chosen their picture, they are to stand in front of it. The director tells them that they will work with this character. They are to take the picture and think about this person for awhile. The actors will need to know a lot about him or her so they should be prepared to ask themselves a lot of questions.

The director gives out character sheets containing the following questions:

1. How old is this character?
2. What sort of attitude does this character project?
3. What is the character thinking about?
4. What are his or her hobbies?
5. What makes this character laugh?
6. What kind of a family does the character come from?
7. What is his or her attitude toward the family?
8. When people talk about this character, what do they say?
9. What do teachers say about this character?
10. What is his or her burning ambition?
11. What most frightens the character?
12. Of what is she or he most proud?
13. What is the character's favorite kind of music?
14. What is the secret that she or he wants no one to discover?
15. If this person were a flower, what flower would she or he be?
16. What is his or her usual mood?
17. What type of picture would this character paint?
18. What are his or her friends like?
19. What do the friends say about this character in their journals?
20. What is the meanest thing this character has done?
21. What is the best thing she or he has done?
22. What does this character wish most for in life?

Actors are given thirty minutes in which to think about their character. Those who finish early form pairs and take turns interviewing each other in role. They are encouraged to use the sheet as a source for questions, and to ask any other questions that will help them learn more about each other's character.

The director now gives the actors another thirty minutes. During this time, they are to write in the role of the character and answer the question, "Who am I?" The director tells them that their writing is private and will not be shared.

At the end of the time, the director brings the actors together. She asks them to work in pairs to devise a scene between their character and his or her reflection, keeping in mind that the reflection has been with the character since they were born and is all-knowing. One partner will play the part of his or her character; the other, the character's mirror image. When finished, they will reverse roles and the second partner will portray his or her character. The partners work together to brainstorm topics of conversation. They want the scenes to have tension so they must choose their topics with care. While the actors work together, the director circulates, asking questions and helping out where necessary.

4. PRESENTATION

The partners take turns performing their scenes. The rest of the group serves as the audience and comments on the presentations. The director asks the audience to focus on these questions:

1. Who are these people?
2. How would you describe their relationship?
3. What went on between them?
4. How effective were the actors in conveying this?
5. What would you say the scene was about?
6. What techniques did the actors use to get their ideas across?
7. What do you think of their behavior?
8. How interesting was the performance for the audience?
9. What was successful about the performance?
10. How could the actors have created more tension or surprise?

5. TRANSCRIBING

The director records the scenes on a tape recorder, although this task can be done easily by one of the actors. Later, the scenes will be presented in hard copy for the actors to edit and workshop further.

This outline illustrates two techniques: using a song as a springboard into scenes, and using photographs and pictures as a springboard into creating character. "People" scenes lend themselves to having the actors enter into the role of the characters to be explored while abstract or painting "scenes" lend themselves to interpretation by actors in movement or more abstract ways.

Playbuilding from Shakespeare

The following pages outline how one class of eleven- and twelve-year-olds worked with Portia's story from "The Merchant of Venice." This method works equally well with secondary school students.

STORY OVERVIEW

A wealthy heiress, Portia is constrained by the terms of her father's will in that she cannot choose her own husband. All of her suitors must choose from among a selection of gold, silver, and lead caskets. In one of these caskets is a portrait of Portia, and whoever selects this casket will become her husband. Within each casket, there is also a scroll that rewards the suitor with either a recommendation or an admonishment. Each suitor must promise that if he chooses the wrong casket, he will: (1) leave immediately, (2) keep his choice of casket a secret, and (3) never seek the hand of any other woman in marriage. The drama of the story rests on the many suitors whom Portia dislikes and whom she fears may choose the right casket. Bassanio, Portia's love, chooses the correct casket – the lead one – thereby demonstrating the wisdom of her father's will.

INTRODUCING THE STORY

The director narrates the story in a "Once upon a time, happily ever after style." As well, she outlines the story's key elements including Portia's love for Bassanio, her father's will, the suitors, the caskets, and the "happily ever after" ending.

DISCUSSION

The director initiates a discussion following the telling of the story. She asks, "Does this only happen in fairytales? Do you know of other stories like this?" The discussion centres on how marriage partners are chosen in various cultures, and how these ways differ from our westernized view of romance and marriage.

SYMBOLS

The director asks the actors to think about the caskets and what they symbolize. The different qualities of gold, silver, and lead are discussed, and some students decide to research the differences between these metals. They discover physical information, as well as the idea that lead is used for practical things while gold and silver are used for ornamentation. Together, the group discusses the pliability of lead.

DESIGNING

The class divides into two groups. The director gives each group the same assignment: designing and making three caskets built to protect something precious.

IMPROVISING

The director asks one member from each group to take on the role of Portia and another to take on the role of her dying father. She instructs the groups to create a ritualized ceremony where the casket and her father's will are given to Portia. As well, she gives each group the line "I may neither choose who I would, nor refuse who I dislike" from the play and asks them to incorporate it into the scene. The actors perform their improvisations and discuss what they have seen.

HOT SEAT

In turn, each of the Portias are put on the hot seat to answer questions from the rest of the actors about her feelings for her recently dead father and the will he drew up before he died. The director instructs the group to discover how Portia feels about the will and whether she thinks that she and Bassanio will ever marry. The director encourages the actors to question Portia about her fears concerning the caskets.

VOICE COLLAGE

The director asks the two actors playing Portia to create a verbal collage using some of the words and phrases from the hot seat exercise. The director also introduces other words and phrases from the play script to assist them with this task.

SCULPTURES

The director asks the rest of the group to take on the role of a suitor who wants to marry Portia (outlined in Act 1, scene 2), or to take on the role of a suitor of their own creation. On the director's command, the actors take turns adopting a sculptured pose that tells of their character. Other students examine each pose, and discuss characteristics exhibited by the pose. Students also comment on whether Portia's father would have approved of the various suitors.

MOVING SCULPTORS

The actors select a number of suitors who they think might impress Portia. Each of the selected suitors must now develop a walk that is appropriate to the character. The director sets up a mimed scene with Portia and the caskets. In turn, each suitor enters the scene, responds to Portia, and examines the caskets before exiting.

MUSIC

The director asks the group to consider the type of music that should accompany the mimed scene. The actors explore possibilities and discuss the intended effects on the audience. The director then introduces the words from the song in Act 3, scene 2, "Tell Me Where Is Fancy Bred?" The director explains that in Shakespeare's play the song is sung while Bassanio makes his choice.

The actors form three groups in which they will compose or improvise a tune for this song. Once they have had sufficient time, they present their tune to the other groups. All students then experiment with using the songs as a background to the mimed "suitors scene."

The director reminds the actors that three characters – Morocco, Aragon, and Bassanio – elected to make a choice and mentions the casket each chose. The actors end this section with an important discussion that explores the stereotypical nature of these characters. The discussion helps the actors to see how stereotypes affect our responses.

STILL IMAGE

Actors remain in their three groups. Each group is assigned one of the three characters and devises two still images depicting the moment of choice by one of these characters, and the moment of realization on opening the casket. Each group shows their still images to the others. A discussion follows each presentation.

DISCUSSION

The three groups discuss the degree of dramatic tension in the first moment and how this can be enhanced. They decide that slowing the choice will enhance the tension, as will making a choice for one casket, then another, and another. After the director reminds them about Portia's presence, the actors suggest that incorporating looks between Portia and the suitors may create more tension. The groups discuss the moment of realization and how this changes the focus of the scene. Time is given for the groups to rework their still images to show increased dramatic tension in the first moment and clearer focus in the second. The director tells the groups to present their two depictions in the mode of freeze (still picture) –

dissolve – (group moves to new positions) – freeze. She also suggests that they freeze for five seconds, take five seconds to dissolve to the next freeze, and then freeze again. The groups show each other their work, and discuss the effectiveness of each for the audience.

ALTER EGO

The director asks the groups to bring their still images to life, using an alter ego for each suitor.

In this exercise, an actor becomes the thoughts and feelings of the character and speaks them out loud, for example: "Ah, dear Portia, I must make this important decision slowly, your patience please. . . Alter Ego: Why am I always so indecisive? If I weren't such a wimp, I'd make a bold choice. She's probably seen through me already." Using alter ego has the effect of presenting the character's inner and outer self to the audience, and requires the actors to think more deeply about the character and his or her motivations.

Each group presents the alter ego scene; the director encourages discussion of these inner thoughts and feelings. The discussion centres on the suitability of the inner thoughts for each suitor, and the types of feelings and thoughts humans experience when faced with important choices.

IMPROVISING DIALOGUE

Working in the same three groups, each group elects one actor to play Portia and a second actor to play the suitor. A third actor becomes the three caskets. The director reminds the actors of the inscriptions, and tells them to keep these in mind during the next exercise. The actors improvise dialogue between the suitor and each of the caskets, and between the suitor and Portia. When ready, the groups share and discuss their improvisations.

UTILIZING SHAKESPEARE'S LINES

The director introduces some lines from Shakespeare's play, for example, "Mislike me not for my complexion" and "To my heart's hope! gold, silver, and base lead." She demonstrates how to read to the end of each line of blank verse in order to keep the rhythm and to emphasize the imagery. After the actors experiment with the reading of the lines, they reform their groups and practise their scenes, incorporating some of the lines from Shakespeare's play.

DANCE

The director explains that Shakespeare's plays often ended with a dance. She asks each group to choreograph a dance that might be a successful completion of this love story.

During this time, the whole class has experimented with Shakespeare's story, while delving into the original play. They have deepened their understanding of the characters and the situations involved in the casket story from the "Merchant of Venice," as well as developed skill in the speaking of blank and rhymed verse. They have been involved in storytelling, improvisation, still images, alter ego, soundscape, and voice collage. Even if the work is not presented, the actors have taken part in a lively learning experience.

BUILDING THE PLAY

The director decides on the following order for presenting the play to an audience.

Scene 1: The ritual. Portia's father hands over the will and the caskets.
Scene 2: Portia's feelings are expressed in a voice collage.
Scene 3: Mimed parade of suitors.
Scene 4: Morocco chooses – improvised scene.
Scene 5: Mimed parade of suitors.
Scene 6: Aragon chooses – improvised scene.
Scene 7: Mimed parade of suitors.
Scene 8: Bassanio chooses – improvised scene.
Scene 9: Celebration dance.

CASTING, REHEARSING, AND PRESENTING

The director casts the roles based on observations made during the playbuilding process. The actors rehearse and present the play to an audience comprising other groups involved in similar ventures.

The presentation is part of a festival that has brought together groups of elementary school students who have been working with the plays of Shakespeare. The festival aims to introduce students to Shakespeare and to allow them to develop their own versions of his stories, using the text to enhance their work.

The project uses six love stories and allows actors to explore differing aspects of falling in love. Six stories from four plays are used:

1. The casket story from "The Merchant of Venice."
2. The lover's story from "Love's Labours Lost."
3. The lover's story from "A Midsummer Night's Dream."
4. Oberon and Titania from "A Midsummer Night's Dream."
5. "Romeo and Juliet."
6. Pyramus and Thisbe from "A Midsummer Night's Dream."

The elementary schools that took part in the festival chose one of the stories and used similar playbuilding techniques to develop a fifteen-minute playbuilt play. Although some of the original lines of Shakespeare were used, the plays were not a rendition of the original script, but rather an original play built from Shakespeare's work. From historical evidence, this reflects in part the way Shakespeare developed his plays at the Globe Theatre.

Television – Yes or No? A Playbuilt Play Exploring the Topic of Television

A group of eighteen young actors between the ages of twelve and seventeen chose the topic of television for a playbuilding project. Group members did not know each other when the project began and while some were very experienced at playbuilding, more than half the group had never playbuilt before.

The process, which took eight hours, was divided into four sessions of two hours each. We have described one part session and one full session on the following pages, each illustrating an important aspect of playbuilding.

The Introductory Session (one hour)

The director asks the actors to sit in a circle. She tells them that they are going to create a collaborative play in eight hours that will be viewed by friends and family. When she asks them if they think they can do this, they agree. They put the chairs aside so they can participate in some "get to know you activities." The first of these is the cocktail party.

1. THE COCKTAIL PARTY

The director asks the actors to form two equal groups. The groups face each other from opposite sides of the room. Each person is to find someone from the other group that she or he does not know. On the signal "Go," the actors run to the person they do not know. If someone else reaches a person first, the other person must find another. Once they have a partner, the actors talk to each other to find out as much as possible about the other person. The room is noisy with talk and laughter. After a few minutes, the director signals the actors to return to their line. The activity is repeated three more times, so everyone has a chance to meet at least four new people in the group.

Observe those who "go for their objective" and those who wait for someone to pick them. The game has implications for acting in that it is about pursuing objectives. I relate these games to acting so the group can make the connection.

Actors now form a circle. One member steps into the middle of the circle, and the others tell what they have learned about him or her during the course of the game. The activity continues until all actors have had a chance to step into the middle of the circle.

This can be a revealing exercise when people realize the effects of self-consciousness or nervousness on their ability to listen and remember. Remind actors that good listening skills are vital to acting.

2. LINE UPS

Actors are given ten seconds in which to line themselves up according to age and area where they live (nearest to farthest from playbuilding spot). They then form groups according to favorite foods – the trick in this activity is that the actors must communicate through a means other than speech.

Both of these games – the cocktail party and the line-ups – are ideal beginning games. The physical aspect of the activities lessens self-consciousness and encourages the actors to mix quickly.

Actors sit in a circle and introduce themselves using the following pattern: I'm _____ and I love _____ but I hate _____ . At the end of this game, the director offers twenty-five cents to the person who can repeat everyone's name.

These games took up the first hour of the session. At the end of this hour, members had established an easy rapport. They knew one another's names and had spoken with most of the other group members. They were relaxed and were now ready to work on the play.

Creating a Non-Naturalistic Scene

In a previous session, actors completed the following set of one liners:

Television is ....
When I think of television, I ....
In our family, television ....
If I could design television programs for young people, I would .
I wish that television ....
The best thing about television is ....
The worst thing about television is ....

The director explains to the actors that they will work from their previously completed sheets. She then asks the actors to form groups of five or six members. The director hands each actor a sheet and gives the following instructions:

"With other members of your group, read aloud the first statement on the page. Say what comes into your mind. Continue with the second statement, the third statement, and so on. When you have finished, chat about what things struck you as you read the one liners. See if you can get a sense of some strong statements that are being made about television.

"Your group's task is to create a presentation f some or all of the ideas on your sheets. You can do this anyway you like, except there are to be no naturalistic scenes. You might use dance, movement, chants, songs, rap, machines, or soundscapes. I'll give you twenty minutes to do this. During this time, I will circulate and offer help when asked. There is no right or wrong way to do this activity – just start working together and see what you come up with."

All of the groups tackled this task in a different manner. The following description outlines the successful work of one group.

After reading the one-liner sheets, members of one group discuss the fact that they have made almost equal numbers of positive and negative statements about television. An older member of the group mentions that he loved to watch television when he was younger but now finds that his time is taken up with other activities, exercising being one of them. This leads the group into a discussion of exercise and time spent outdoors versus television as an indoor, sedate activity that could be addictive. One of the younger group members admits to watching six or seven hours of television a day, and never doing any outdoor activities. He describes how television "sucked him in."

A more experienced actor takes a leadership role by suggesting that the group experiment with a machine that makes the statement that television is both bad and good. He begins the machine by standing in the centre of the group and chanting "Television is good" while making a mechanical, machine-like movement with his head. His expression is vacant. The rest of the group joins the machine, one by one, chanting either "Television is good" or "Television is bad."

The group discusses their work. Some members think that the scene is good, and that they have done what is required of them. They are ready to present their work to the large group. However, there is an obvious problem – two things are being said at once which makes the meaning of the message unclear. One of the group members mentions that the machine doesn't express important topics or feelings that arose from their one liners and discussions. Another member mentions that it doesn't comment on the addictive element of television, and how time spent watching television limits outdoor and more physical activities. This leads to a discussion of how these elements could be incorporated in the scene.

The young actor who stated earlier that television "sucked him in" becomes excited by the idea of turning the machine into a monster that literally consumes people. One of the group suggests that members could be playing around the machine, which would be chanting "Television is good." One by one, actors would stop playing, become curious about the machine, and would suddenly be consumed by it. They would then form part of the machine until it was all encompassing. No actors would be left, and the machine would continue its chant of "Television is good." The group works on the scene, and eventually presents it to the large group where it receives an enthusiastic response.

This group completed the process without the assistance of the director. One of the more experienced members took over as leader, asking questions and encouraging other members to clarify their ideas. Experienced in playbuilding, he readily accepted the ideas of the other members and used questions to push them to think more deeply. Given his expertise, it was not necessary for the director to step in and prod the group by asking questions or having them return to their original source of material – the one liners.

Of the three pieces shown that day, all members of the group voted unanimously that the machine scene be included in their play. Later, the director would find an opportunity to include all eighteen actors in this part of the play. Although the work of the other groups was rejected for further development, the actors reacted well because they were excited by the prospects of the machine scene.

During the creation of a play, the director needs to be on the lookout for scenes where the whole cast can be utilized on stage.

The director now works with the entire group to:

- place the actors (the stage picture). Eighteen actors is a lot to have on stage at one time. The director places the machine centre stage (the strongest position), and arranges the other actors into four groups around the machine. Each group engages in a different outdoor activity. Time is spent polishing the mime performance so that the physical activities, for example, catching and throwing balls, are synchronized.
- create tension. The director slows the approach of the actors to the machine to ensure that there are distinct moments. As an example, the first actor is stopped in his game by the machine. He approaches the machine to investigate. He says his line, and the machine focuses on the actor before becoming animal-like and reaching out to "devour" the actor. Slowing the action is necessary to build tension; it is the director's job to oversee the timing of stage action.
- introduce dialogue. The director decides that it would add

to the tension if there is more dialogue with the machine. She takes some of the one-liner statements and gives them to various actors. The machine begins its chant, "Television is good." An actor stops playing, approaches, and listens a minute. She says, "No it isn't, because there's too much violence."

- highlight the dramatic elements. The reaching out motion and the sucking sound have to be "big." Time is spent on the movement of the "tentacles" and the enlargement of the sucking sound.
- time the ending. The director decides how many "Television is good" lines will be most dramatic once all the actors have been consumed. She decides that three work best, followed by silence.

When the play was shown to an invited audience, this section became the focus of much discussion. Non-naturalistic pieces are thought-provoking because they, like abstract paintings, are open to interpretation. They create opportunities for both the cast and the audience to think metaphorically.

5

G'Day Sport

This chapter describes a major playbuilding project that took one term to complete. The group worked together for approximately three hours per week; the directors spent two weeks on initial research. First performed in Sydney, Australia, the play was later revised and presented at the Youth Theatre Festival in Newcastle, Australia.

PROJECT SETTING

The cast comprised a class of students enrolled in an integrated program at a high school of performing arts. The school has programs in dance, drama, music, visual arts, and ballet. Students enrolled in the integrated program must take a one-term course in drama that focuses on developing and performing a play.

THE ACTORS

There were twenty-two students in the group, between fifteen and eighteen years of age. All of the students were new to the school, having successfully completed an audition for entrance that year. There were three male students and nineteen female students in the group. While all had experience in performing plays and dance, none had experience in playbuilding. When they came together to do this project, they did not know one another.

THE CONTEXT

Because the students were interested in the arts and particularly in dance, they did not have a strong interest in other sports.

Their previous schools, however, had a policy where all students had to participate in at least one competitive sport. The students decided to explore the issue of sport through a play.

ASSESSMENT

Student assessment for the term was based on their contribution to the presentation, as well as on the skills they displayed as individual performers. Students were required to keep a logbook that documented their involvement in the presentation.

Because the work was a required part of the curriculum, students were focused and keen to engage in the process. Although two teacher/directors were assigned to the group, one was also responsible for other groups and as a consequence could devote only a limited amount of time to the project.

Stage One: Exploring

The directors offer the actors a chance to form small groups in which they can develop a play. The actors discuss this choice, but elect to work as a whole group. The reasons for this choice, they explain to the directors, lie in the fact that they do not know one another. They hope that through working in a large group, they can cement relationships with a number of fellow actors.

This decision has some far-reaching implications. The play will have to include all twenty-two actors, and provide for all of them the opportunity to show their skills as a performer. It means, too, that there is little possibility for role doubling since twenty-two roles in any performance is plenty. The directors reason that there are several approaches that can be taken to accommodate such a large group: (1) setting the play in an institution such as a school, and (2) using a collage format in which a number of roles can be linked thematically. The directors know that this latter method will not be the best way for these actors to work since, at this stage, they have little experience of dramatic forms other than a narrative sequence.

The Ideas Circle

The directors ask the actors to form a circle. They explain to the actors that the play can be about any topic, issue, or concern that they would like to explore. The directors outline reasons why the topic must appeal to all actors, and warn them that this task is more difficult than first assumed.

The actors can record their topics and throw them into the circle for discussion. The directors explain that they will not impose limitations on the topics the actors raise – this will be a group process where all members will have to make decisions. The directors stipulate one condition, however, and that is that actors respond to the topic and not to the actor who has raised it or read it aloud.

This was quite easy as the actors had not developed strong feelings – positive or negative – toward one another. They had, to this point, concentrated on improvisational work and were still fairly flexible in their groupings.

Actors suggest a number of topics – sex, fashion, peer pressure, drugs – that are met with a variety of responses ranging from immediate rejection to luke-warm enthusiasm. This continues until one actor throws the idea of sport into the ring.

The effect of this was magnetizing. Like the effect of a pebble thrown into a pond, there was a moment of stillness and then ripples began to move outward. There was an overwhelming acceptance of this idea on the part of all actors, and the buzz of excitement was infectious. It seemed that all of them had a story related to sports.

The Story Circle

The directors ask the actors to form groups of three. With their group members, actors share their best and worst story about sport. After all group members have shared their stories, the directors ask each group to select one of their stories and prepare a retelling of it for the other groups. All members take part in the retelling.

These retellings were strong – the vehemence with which these actors disliked competitive sport culture was amazing. It was obvious that the group had a lot to say on this topic.

Some of the stories are quite comic, and one retelling is particularly funny. The group experiments with it as a scene, but finds that some of the humor is lost. One actor suggests that it be tried as a monologue, and it works well.

The monologue is delivered by a character called Frank, a tomboy who refuses to use her full name, Francesca, and whose main interests in life are soccer and other male sports. Frank has a friend called Ashley, who admires and basks in the aura of Frank's "butch" manner. The monologue is set in the context of a drama class story circle.

FRANK: Yeah, well – see this happened in the hols. Me brother went down to this soccer camp – lucky devil – and dad and me went down for the invitation match on the last day, and someone on their team had an accident and so they were down one player. So me brother tells the coach – I got a mate come down to see the match. He's a real good player, and the coach falls over himself and sends me brother to get this mate so they won't lose the match. An' the coach when he sees me says, you look like a real tough player. We need to win this match, right. He was a bit short-sighted see – couldn't tell I was not a guy. So the game begins, you see, and this team of me brothers, they're a pretty soft lot – and the other team's pretty tough and they c'n move with the ball – no wonder the coach was worried. So I play real hard – and just before the end of the match I score two goals – wow!
Anyway we get back to the change room and the coach comes in to give the team a pep talk – you know like this – you do it Ashley.

ASHLEY: Right you load of pansies. I watched you out there on that field. You were playing like a team of prissy little girls making daisy chains. There wasn't one 'f you that looks like a real soccer player – 'cept for Frank here. Now if he hadn't come down today you'd have been firmly trounced. Take note – all you would be soccer champs — you can't play soccer like it's a game of marbles. Soccer is a real man's game, and if you want to play it you gotta be tough like Frank. Here's a boy what'll grow up to be a champion soccer player, not like the rest of you pansies.

Actors identify and sort some of the scenes according to theme. These include the maleness of sport, the pressure that parents put on young people to win, and the drive to compete that is not only about playing the game, but also about conquering the opponent and winning the trophy.

Improvisations

The directors ask the actors to work in small groups. In their groups, they select one of the themes and improvise a scene that makes a statement about it. The scene can be naturalistic or non-naturalistic. The directors encourage the actors to experiment and explore through enactment rather than further discussion. When the groups have created their scene, the directors ask them to recreate it through the use of a different setting, changing the characters, or experimenting to see whether any problems would be better handled another way.

Each group then selects one improvisation and prepares it for presentation to the other actors. Time is allowed for groups to work and rework the scenes they have created. The presentations are made to the whole group, and are followed up with further discussions of the issues presented.

Some of the presentations did not take the actors much further than the stereotypes presented in some of the stories. Others, however, showed considerable development of ideas.

The directors work with some of the groups who are having difficulty. They help the actors tighten the dialogue and explore with them how they can develop a focus for the scene.

The reworked scenes are presented to the other actors. One scene involves an argument between a coach and a parent over training practices. The argument is transformed into two monologues, one of which follows:

TRACEY: There's my mother. . . can't wait to the holidays, so she can supervise my training herself. Doesn't trust the coach to do it properly. Pays him a fortune, but practically takes over herself. Three carnivals she enters me in. . . so it's training night and morning. I mean, there I was, thinking that at least for the holidays I'd be able to sleep in. . . but no! It's up at five, my breakfast already on the table, gulp it down, and

---

> then to the pool, and diving in, the water's freezing, but we can't train in the heated pool, oh no, that would soften up the muscles. . . so in we go, tearing down the end of the pool, breathing every four strokes, and each time I look up, there she is running down the side, with a flamin' stop watch in her hand, counting the flamin' seconds. . . tumble turn at the end, and head down for the blocks and this time I look up and it's the coach, you know, running down the other side, yellin' somethin' about the curve of my foot or arm or something. Never does that when my mother's not there. . .

The discussion of the scenes elicits comments about the language of sport, particularly its aggressiveness, and how sports commentators and others seem to need to yell the words at people. This shouting seems to be a part of the actors' experiences of sports teachers, and several of the scenes feature experiences where they were coached through a megaphone or some similar device. The actors discuss one of the scenes that contains good material, but has some structural problems. They decide to try it as a monologue. In this form, it would later serve as the play's climax.

> SOULA: Bradman is going to win the trophy again. . . get rid of all those frivolous thoughts floating around in your minds. No excuses now. Right. Ready. On your marks. . . Wait for the whistle. Get set. Get the adrenaline pumping. (Whistle) Now keep a steady pace in the first lap. Don't fall back behind the pack. Keep up. Let's see some real energy. . . keep the power flowing. . . don't drop back. . . keep with the pack. . . You're slipping behind the rest. . . get up with them. Good Frank. . . out in front now as you head for the hurdles. Don't drop your back foot Kelly or you'll clip the hurdle. Keep your head up Ashley. . . Who is that at the end?. . . C'mon you stupid girl. . .

Actors are familiar with the language of sport, having heard it repeatedly in their former schools. One of the improvised scenes centres on a school assembly. The scene is first presented with actors playing the parts of the assembly and with much interaction between the students and teachers on the assembly platform. The actors decide to change this to a presentational dialogue with the audience serving as the students in the assembly.

GRETAL: 'Morning teams. This is your captain speaking. . .

JO: And Vice. . .

GRETAL: Welcome Back. Feeling trim, taut, and terrific? Last term was a winning innings and this term we're gonna hit 'em for six.

JO: And rip 'em and bash 'em and slay 'em. . .

GRETAL: I'll be at the helm leading the way to victory, and you, my faithful little teammates will work, strive, and train. . .

JO: Until the regional trophy is in our hands.

MISS CRANNY: Thank you Gretal. . . Jo. It is no wonder with such a fine captain that Bradman High has been on top for the last five terms. So, as this term begins, remember to work hard and aim high. Remember our school motto is – Strive to Win.

Stage Two: Framing

The group meets to discuss and plan the next stage. There is more material than can possibly be incorporated within a single play so it is necessary to focus the work and find a source of dramatic tension that can be sustained through the narrative. Both these aspects fall into place once the next crucial decision is made by the group.

As the actors discuss the scenes that have been explored or presented, it becomes obvious that almost all focus on school experiences of sport and involve students, parents, or teachers. They agree that the play needs to be set in a high school. Discussion of the type of high school ranges widely until one actor suggests that the school be a replica of their own, but should specialize in sports achievement. This suggestion is accepted by the group.

The actors want to give the school a name, and the choice of Bradman is agreed to after a number of alternatives are considered. The actors don't know a great deal about Bradman, save that he was a famous Australian sports figure. Through research, they discover that Bradman was Sir Donald Bradman, a cricketeer who set many records during his long career and captained many test matches. Bradman symbolizes for the actors the epitome of sports achievement without the "aggro" and "macho" elements that they have encountered in their own schooling experiences.

The next step involves constructing the Bradman High community. The directors ask the actors to record in their logbooks some aspects of their view of the school. They can write entries or sketch their thoughts. They provide the actors with leading questions, for example: Where is the school located? What are its grounds and buildings like? Do the students wear uniforms?

The Sharing Circle

The actors bring their log material – notes, plans, sketches, ideas – to the sharing circle. Considerable discussion of the physical environment of the school ensues. There is a surprising degree of similarity among the actors' perception of the school. They see the buildings as having little architectural interest, notice boards are covered with graffiti, staff rooms are bare and lifeless, school uniforms are shades of browns and maroons, the gymnasium is multipurpose and well-equipped, and the grounds are enormous. Most importantly the school motto – Strive to Win – is agreed upon by all.

These ideas will be translated into a simple set that consists of two revolving flats that represent the walls of different parts of the school, including the staff room, assembly hall, yard, and principal's office.

Having reached a consensus about the issues the play is to explore and the physical setting of the narrative, actors now have to make decisions about the play's characters. The directors ask each actor to choose the type of character she or he wants to portray – staff, parent, or student. Although this decision can be reversed, it is important that as the scenario forms the actors have some idea of character. Actors are equally divided into those that want to play students and teachers. Only two actors, however, are interested in playing the role of parents.

There is some juggling and negotiating at this point. Two actors – one male and one female – want to play the role of the principal. The group discusses the idea of a strong female principal pushing a competitive macho sports ethos. The group debates the issue and creates some improvisations involving male and female principals before they decide to move ahead with the female principal. One of these improvisations, which involves the principal and deputy-principal in a school assembly, will eventually be developed as the assembly scenes in the play.

At this point, it was obvious that the actors had developed a deep commitment to the project. The play gave them a chance to incorporate their personal stories into the fabric of a collaborative work.

Writing Biographies

The directors have the actors write a biography of their character. They ask them to recount the character's experiences and qualities within a school setting. This writing exercise helps the actors give form to their character.

Hot Seat

The actors share their character biographies. To assist in deepening their roles, some actors take the hot seat. The other actors question them about their character and what their role will be in the school. The hot seating exercise establishes the actors' sense of frustration with, and hostility to, the ethos of the school. This is most evident when the actor playing the part of the art teacher takes the hot seat, and the possibility for dramatic tension becomes apparent. Two of the actors who are playing the part of students also discuss their overbearing parents. They become the children of the two actors who want to play the role of parents.

Improvisations

The group returns to improvising mode and divides into two groups. Actors playing staff members work as a group to explore a variety of staff-room situations while actors playing students improvise several scenes on the playground, on the sports field, in the classroom, and around the lockers. Actors playing the parents work with both their children and the staff.

When both groups have had sufficient time to improvise scenes, they meet again as a large group to share their improvisations and discuss the next steps to be taken. There is a plethora of possible scenes, some dramatically interesting, others less so. Although characters have begun to develop alliances, both in the staff room and on the playground, the play still lacks an overall shape.

Stage Three: Sequencing

In this stage, actors must select the scenes to be included in the play, and sequence them in an order which reflects and supports their statement about competitive sport. Until this point, the directors have tended to let the actors control the playbuilding process. At the sequencing stage, however, they take tighter control of the work, finding it necessary to offer direction in this area as the actors' knowledge of dramatic form is not sufficient for the task.

Sociograms

The directors ask the actors to draw up sociograms that will show interactions between the characters, staff, and students. The actors indicate through the drawings the likes and dislikes of each character. The actors share their views of the sociograms and considerable discussion follows. From this, it becomes obvious that the points of conflict are between characters who oppose the ethos of competition and winning and those who are committed to victory at any cost. In the middle are characters who sit on the fence, or who have been victimized by the system.

The actors discuss how the narrative should proceed. They suggest a number of scenarios and explore some of these through improvisation. The focus then shifts to exploring the issue of what occurs when you introduce a foreign or opposing element into a mix that is already unstable. The actors discuss parallels between teachers and students, and it is obvious that clear liaisons have begun to develop between some teachers and students.

The group feels that the dramatic tension has to originate

from two characters. The first is Samantha, an asthmatic, who of all the students is most opposed to the emphasis on sport. The second is the dance/drama teacher, Miss Beth. The actors' decision to add these elements to the mix begins to establish the narrative line, helps to focus the action, and identifies the source of dramatic tension.

The actors agree to the directors' request that they review the scenes in order to select those which have the most dramatic potential and which relate most closely to the group's view of the negative qualities of competitive sport. The actors identify approximately fifteen scenes that they believe meet this criteria. Some of the scenes selected involve the same characters so the actors must determine how much stage time each character will be allotted.

This stage proved quite difficult for many of the actors. Some had personal attachments to the improvisations that had been rejected as less interesting or lacking dramatic potential. The actors' feelings of rejection were difficult to manage at this point because they were multilayered. They involved the actors' connection with previous schools and the associated pain of this connection, their new relationships within the group, and their identification with the characters of the play.

With the directors, the actors have to establish a sequence for the chosen scenes. In an attempt to establish a narrative line, some of the scenes have to be eliminated. Some actors, witnessing the red pen delete their monologue or moment of high drama, feel a sense of loss and angst. This is particularly true in the case of the parents' scenes – the group is having difficulty establishing their position in the play.

The end result of this process is the shaping of a narrative without the full dramatic complication. The actors are firm in their determination that there will be a change in the ethos of Bradman High by the end of the play. They are also set on the idea that this change will be brought about by the newcomers – Samantha, the asthmatic and Miss Beth, the dance/drama teacher. The actors have developed a scene where Samantha, who has been ridiculed because of her asthma, is forced into an activity by a teacher despite a doctor's certificate excusing her from the task. Her life is put at risk by the teacher, Soula, who maintains a single-minded determination to win at all costs.

At this stage, there are some interesting scenes that involve Miss Beth and her students. These scenes provide contrast to the relationship Soula shares with her students. Before these scenes can be finalized, however, the actors need to do more work. They must: establish a close connection between Soula and Miss Beth, explore further the relationships of other staff members, find a place for the parents in the narrative, and establish a stronger crisis point.

Speaking Diary/Hot Seat

The group turns their attention to the relationship between Miss Beth and Soula. Using speaking diary and hot seat, they explore the nature of the enmity between these two characters.

As the actors explored this antipathy, it grew and intensified. The degree to which they had immersed themselves in their roles was evident in their strong response to this activity.

Some of these improvisations prove fruitful, yielding the notion of Miss Beth competing for the students' training time in order to rehearse the school play. At this stage, there is no sense of the topic of the play "within a play." That will come later. In particular, the actors react strongly to one improvised scene. It provides the catalyst for the development of the piece and is developed as a crucial moment in the drama. The scene is as follows:

SOULA: I've been looking for you. This time you've gone too far. I've had it. First I was supposed to get another P.E. teacher. . . and they send me you! And now. . . Well, it's not good enough! You're just going to have to fit into this place, and not try to change it. This school is built on sport. We live sport, and some pretty little ballet teacher is not going to upset my school. I've got pull in this school. . . real power. And if I say jump, they'll jump. . . and if you think you're going to take my star sportsmen to be in some pansy production you can think again, do you hear?

MISS BETH: I pray you Miss Papadopolous, do be calm. I'm sure we can come to some agreement.

SOULA: Are you mad. . . or just deaf. There'll be no agreement. You'll just do as I say.

> MISS BETH: Be merciful, Miss Papadopolous. Surely, you can, in a spirit of generosity and compassion, allow a little time out of training for rehearsals.
>
> SOULA: Generosity! Compassion! You know what you can do with your hoity-toity words and your hoity-toity play. . . You listen and listen good. You cross me over this and it'll be too late to beg for mercy. No play. . . right!

The revenge motif that develops between these two characters elicits stories from the actors concerning observations they have made of teachers who claim curriculum territory within schools. It is a reminder to the directors that students are far more observant of political maneuverings than staff are probably aware. This discussion leads to a revamping of the staffroom scenes in order to bring out other aspects of the political network that operate within them.

The directors ask the actors to observe political maneuverings within their own school. They find the actors' observations of teachers – their voices, movements, and ways of interacting – to be surprisingly accurate.

> MISS DODD: What do you think of this? I'm looking for something to teach the first-year students.
>
> MISS DIOR: Yuk! Looks revolting. . . but I guess they'll like it.
>
> MISS DODD: It's so hard to predict what they're going to like.
>
> MISS DIOR: What else is there?
>
> MISS DODD: Well, there's this flan. . .
>
> MISS DODD: Now that looks gorgeous. . . scrumptious.
>
> MISS DODD: It's quite healthy, too. Oh, it's for a microwave. Have to forget that one. All the interesting recipes seem to be for microwaves. I've been waiting for ours to come for months.
>
> MISS MCWILLIAM: That power hungry beast!
>
> MISS DIOR: Judith, what's the matter?
>
> MISS MCWILLIAM: I've just been informed by our illustrious principal that we won't be purchasing the video camera which I need to cover the media section of the syllabus.
>
> MISS DIOR: What's the problem with the budget this time?

MISS MCWILLIAM: All the funds have been spent on new volleyballs, nets and various other sundry items of sports equipment.

MISS DODD: I suppose that is a change from athletics equipment. I requisitioned a microwave oven at the beginning of the year. I suppose if it could be used to bake something for the teams I'd have a chance of getting it.

MISS MCWILLIAM: Well this is the limit. How can one implement a proper syllabus in this place?

MISS DUBOIS: What's eating Menaly? She looks like she is about to murder someone. . . or incite a riot or rebellion.

MISS DIOR: What's eating her? What's eating all of us? I've got to teach craft this term. Craft means pottery – here – it's written in the syllabus. But how do you do that when you haven't got a kiln? And now I've got to build a set for this drama production without any budget at all, and there isn't a shred of canvas in the art department.

MISS MCWILLIAM: So I'm not the only one with a gripe. . .

MISS DODD: That make's three. . . What about you Renee?

MISS DUBOIS: I don't have anything to complain about. My students are doing well in French. They are all keen to succeed. Sport does not interfere with their work or mine, and I think it does help to motivate them to succeed.

MISS DODD: I just wish we had the pull that Soula does in this school. . .

SOULA: So you don't like sport. . . Menaly tells me you want to spend money on ovens and videos so they can all get fat and lazy and out of form, and then we'll lose a few matches. That's what you all want for Bradman High? No way. I know where you're getting these soft ideas – it's that new teacher. I'll fix her.

MISS DIOR: Soula, down. You have done wonders for this school. No one denies that, but you're being such a. . . such a. . . bully.

SOULA: Bully! I'll give you bully. I'll fix Miss Beth and the lot of you in one go!

The obvious intertextual references in the duologue between Soula and Miss Beth come into this scene a little later as the group agonizes over whether they need to let the audience know the topic of the play within the play. This discussion sparks an argument about whether it should be something that would be seen as fun, such as a Broadway musical, or whether it should give a message to the audience that what the actors are doing in the drama is important and serious. They opt for the latter, and then have to make a decision about which play they will choose.

The choice of Shakespeare is unanimous. The actors, who have only a sketchy knowledge of Shakespeare, perceive his plays to be serious and therefore obviously important! Most of the actors admit that they do not understand Shakespeare, but this is not important as one can write essays on his work through the use of explanatory notes.

By chance, some of the actors are introduced to "The Merchant of Venice" in their English class. Needless to say, the study of Shakespeare in a performing arts school differs greatly from what most of the actors had experienced in their previous schools. As their study of the play progresses, the actors begin to make connections between what is happening in their play and the issues presented in "The Merchant of Venice," particularly justice and fair play.

They also connect with Shylock's revenge and decide that this fits well with Soula's behavior in the school. They decide that she is a vengeful character who will punish Miss Beth for the growing popularity of drama that is wooing Soula's champions away from sport.

Thus the choice of a scene for rehearsal is made easy – the court scene from "The Merchant of Venice" raises these issues. As well, it provides the opportunity to introduce the idea of potential physical injury – a premonition of the physical injury that will follow in the final scene. This is reinforced by having Samantha play the part of Antonio, and by the insertion of bridger lines. The scene becomes:

ASHLEY/SHYLOCK: My deeds upon my head: I crave the law. The penalty and forfeit of my bond.
JENNY/PORTIA: Is he not able to discharge the money?
KIM/BASSANIO: Yes, here I tender it for him in the court.
Yea, twice the sum: if that will not suffice
I will be bound to pay it ten times over.
If this will not suffice, it must appear
That malice bears down truth. And I beseech you
Wrest once the law to your authority
To do a great right, do a little wrong
And curb this devil of his will.

SAM: What's Bassanio trying to do there?

MISS BETH: Bassanio is trying to get Portia to change the rules to suit Antonio's case. . . and Portia is saying that nothing can alter a law.

SAM: That's like this place.

MISS BETH: What do you mean?

SAM: Well the law in this place is sport – compulsory sport – and nothing will alter that!

MISS BETH: Things do change Sam – sometimes more slowly than we would like, perhaps. . .

ASHLEY/SHYLOCK: A Daniel come to judgement. . .
O wise young judge, how I do honour thee!

JENNY/PORTIA: Be merciful. . .
Take thrice thy money and bid me tear the bond.

ASHLEY/SHYLOCK: By my soul I swear
There is no power in the tongue of man
to alter me.

SAM/ANTONIO: Most heartily I do beseech the court
To give the judgement.

Enter Frank

FRANK: 'Scuse me Miss, but Miss Papadopalous sent me to tell you that she needs all the Year 10's for track training now – or else!

SAM: We can't come yet, we. . .

FRANK: She's real mad and she'll make you go round a hundred times if you don't come now. . . she'll make you run till you drop. . .

This stage in the process brings the group to a situation where the scenario is complete. Actors decide that the story will be told in chronological order. The characters are defined, and the actors feel comfortable sustaining the character they have developed.

Synopsis – G'Day Sport

The play is set within the context of the high school, with all but two scenes occurring on the premises. The school is returning from the vacation, and those students who revel in competitive sport are keen to begin the round of competitions. They put pressure on all students to participate. We meet Samantha, a new student and an asthmatic, who is not very interested in sport and who is derided by some of the more aggressive students. There are some students, however, who are less than keen, and we meet two of these, Tracey, a swimmer and Kenneth, a tennis player. We also meet Tracey's mother and Kenneth's father and see that some parents, at least, are very happy that the school places such importance on winning competitions.

At the school assembly, we meet the principal and deputy-principal, as well as the school sports captain and vice-captain. The ethos of winning is further reinforced. We then meet the new teacher who has been assigned to the school, and in place of the hoped-for physical education teacher, there is a drama/dance teacher. From the responses of the principal, deputy-principal, and other staff we realize that trouble will be brewing here.

As the students also get wind of the news, they reveal their attitudes about prissy subjects, and the tension increases further. We become aware of the strong bond that Soula, the sports mistress, has used to control the students and the power that she wields in the school.

We visit the first drama lesson and find that Miss Beth is no fool, and that she has done her homework on the students in her class.

Visits from the two parents to the principal indicate the growing tension between the ideals of competitive sport and the drama work, and we also see the uncaring pressure that is put on students to push themselves to the limit physically.

The tension in the school is further increased when some of the staff are thwarted in their attempts to have funds spent on resources for their subject areas, while unlimited funds are diverted to the purchase of sports equipment.

The injustices within the school come to a head through the play within the play that is being rehearsed by Miss Beth. The students are coming to see that there is more to school than competitive sport. The interruption of the rehearsal for a training session is brought to an abrupt end by the collapse of Samantha on the field, with a severe bout of asthma, an event that causes everyone to re-evaluate their positions.

The conflict is resolved by accommodating other viewpoints apart from competitive sport.

It is now a matter of sequencing the chosen scenes in chronological order. Having established the scenario, the directors and actors can develop links between the scenes.

1. The school yard – students return after holidays
2. Tracey's home – mother monologue
3. The school yard – students after holidays
4. Kenneth's father – monologue – dictating letter
5. The school yard – students after holidays
6. School hall – assembly
7. Principal's office – the new teacher arrives
8. Staff room – the new teacher is introduced
9. Playing fields – the sports teacher and students
10. Classroom – drama teacher takes a class
11. Principal's office – Tracey's mother complains
12. School yard – students
13. Principal's office – Kenneth's father complains
14. Staff room complaints
15. School yard – students
16. Staff room – Miss Beth vs Soula
17. Classroom – rehearsal
18. Sports field – monologue
19. Staff room – aftermath
20. Assembly – monologue

The sequence also reveals that there is a need for strong opening and closing scenes to frame the narrative. The directors and actors decide that both these scenes should be choreographed as dance routines. The closing scene is choreographed as a rap dance. As the dance proceeds, the staff is gradually drawn into the dance, including Soula, who finds (reluctantly) that it is physical and energetic.

The opening scene is more difficult to devise, since the group has to find a suitable piece of music. A number of pieces are suggested and tried out, but they do not work. The breakthrough finally comes during one of the rehearsals. One of the actors uses an Australian term that is associated with being a good sport – come on Aussie, come on. The group incorporates this term in a song, and the spontaneous use of the phrase seems to focus the opening of the play.

The appropriateness of this song as a piece that will set the scene is obvious. The group decides to write words for the song that introduce the main characters, and to choreograph it so that the characters' identities are established from the opening moment of the play.

> We've been training all the winter
> And there's not a team that's fitter
> and that's the way it's got to be
> We're up against the best you know
> This is regional sports you know
> And you've gotta be the best the school has seen
> Soula is the leader of the Teams
> Soula is the heart in our machines
> The parents are the pits
> And Cranny's having fits
> And Bradley's eyes have got that killer gleam
> Miss Beth's playing havoc with the bats
> Gretal and Jo, it's good to see you back
> Kelly's on the run an' Frank's chewing gum
> And Kenneth's slicin' them down like an axe
>
> Come on Aussie come on, come on
> Come on Bradman come on, come on
> Come on Aussie come on, come on
> Come on Bradman come on, come on.
>
> Tracey she is swimmin' like a laser
> Yeh I'm another Dawn Fraser
> Sam is an asthmatic
> And the staff's gettin' frantic
>
> And Bradman High We're gonna hit the skies
> Yeah
> Come on Aussie come on, come on
> Come on Bradman come on, come on
> Repeat ad lib

Stage Four: Rehearsing

The rehearsal stage begins with the directors scripting the workshopped pieces and distributing the scripts to the actors.

Some actors were upset to find that some of their favorite lines had been transformed or omitted. However, they realized that they could still change some of the lines or scenes through the short rehearsal process.

Making Decisions about the Set

At this stage, the directors decide that as little furniture as possible will be used. This decision is in part determined by the fact that the play will have to travel to at least two venues. Two flats on wheels will be used as the backdrop to the action. They will be swung around to indicate different locations.

One side of each flat is painted with a neutral color that allows it to represent scenes that involve the staff room, assembly hall, principal's office, and the parents of two students. Various pictures, mirrors, notice boards, and so on are hung from hooks, the location of which varies to indicate different rooms. The other side of each flat is painted bright yellow and covered with graffiti. This side is used for all student scenes in the school yard.

Scene changes consist of a revolution of the flats. In rehearsing these scene changes, the group decides to use music, and so a search is conducted to find selections that link and comment on the scenes. This is a relatively easy process.

Individual scenes are rehearsed with the two directors taking responsibility for particular scenes. The rehearsal techniques use improvisation and other strategies to focus the dramatic moments. Many of the scenes fall quickly into place as they have come out of a great deal of exploratory improvisation. The realistic form also assists the actors in developing each scene. Hot seating is a common way of dealing with any problems in relation to characters.

The play within the play is workshopped by rehearsing the court scene from "The Merchant of Venice" so that actors are familiar with the issues and how they relate to their play.

Much of the rehearsal time, however, is concerned with the mechanics of the production. It is important that in this narrative structure, the momentum is not lost between scenes. Consequently, particular emphasis is given to the ways in which the flats are turned, and to the placement of any chairs or benches that are needed. These pieces are the only furniture used, and some time is spent in rehearsing ways of moving them on and off stage as quickly as possible.

Since there is no possibility of lighting changes for the initial production, the actors must move in time to the music, which is being used to set the scene. The complete visibility of all changes makes it important that they are done in a way that communicates something further to the audience. The swinging to and fro of the flats begins to take on a life of their own as they shift the audience from one side of the argument to the other.

Stage Five: Performing

This play is performed in three venues. All are school hallways of various shapes and sizes. The performances occur on the floor space rather than on a raised stage. None of the halls has facilities that allow for changes in lighting. The audiences are arranged in a wide semi-circle around the performing space.

The actors, in costume, greet the audience and complete the front of house work in role. The signal for beginning is a musical cue that leads into the opening routine of "Aussie, c'mon." The players gradually join in from where they are in the auditorium, eventually grouping themselves on the stage for the final chorus.

Similarly, the rap dance at the end is rehearsed with a curtain call that allows the actors to exit, still dancing, through the audience. This achieves an interesting bonding, particularly with the students in the audience, many of whom tell the actors of their own competitive sports stories after the play is completed. A number of audience members express a desire to have the opportunity to do more arts subjects in their schools.

The play has a running time of one hour with no intermission. It has taken eleven weeks to develop, with the bulk of the time being spent on developing the work. As is true for almost all playbuilt plays, the rehearsing time is minimal.

The first round of performances occurs at the end of the eleven weeks. The third performance occurs some weeks later, in a city one hundred miles from the actors' home town. Given their other commitments, there is time for only one rehearsal of three hours before the final performance. Most of this rehearsal is devoted to ensuring the mechanical aspects of the production are smoothly effected.

The actors slide easily into their characters for this performance. Their commitment to them has been so strongly established through the playbuilding process that this is an easy transition for them.

The project is a satisfying one for the actors. Their reflections and logbooks reveal the depth of their learning about themselves, other people, and the world around them. It has been a challenge for most of actors, and they would like the chance to engage in another similar project.

6

Immigrant stories

This chapter describes a major playbuilding project that took
three terms to complete. The group worked approximately six
hours a week for fifteen weeks (94 hours). The director spent
sixteen hours on initial research before the cast was chosen.
The play was later adapted for an Australian youth theatre
necessitating further research, the collection of stories from
Australian English as a Second Language students, and the adap-
tation of Canadian stories where appropriate. This description
is of the Canadian project, with some comments on the
Australian version.

THE SETTING
The play was developed at an urban, non-profit youth theatre.
The rehearsals were held after school and on weekends.

THE ACTORS
Eighteen young actors were chosen based on the success of their
audition. They ranged in age from twelve to nineteen years old;
the average age was fifteen. The cast was drawn from a variety
of ethnic backgrounds, including Chinese, Maltese, East Indian,
South American, Filipino, Japanese, Malaysian, French, Italian,
German, Scottish, Irish, Welsh, and English. With the exception of three people, the actors were experienced in
playbuilding, having attended the youth theatre for an average
of three years. Of the three inexperienced actors, two were ESL
students.

The writer/director for this project, an immigrant to Canada, had a long-standing interest in cultural integration, race relations, and ESL students. A former ESL teacher, she had used drama as one way to teach English. She wanted to create this play with a group of young people in an effort to help combat racism and promote understanding of other cultures. This project is an example of playbuilding based on a director-chosen topic. The young actors who auditioned for the project knew in advance the topic of the play.

PROJECT DEVELOPMENT

The project was divided into three stages:
Stage One: Director's Research (16 hours)
Stage Two: Actors' Research and Playbuilding (82 hours)
Stage Three: Rehearsal and Performance (12 hours)

Stage One: Director's Research

The director and her assistant began the play by holding workshops with two groups of inner-city elementary and secondary school ESL students. All students had been chosen by their school for inclusion in the project, and were able to discuss, in English, their experiences of coming to Canada.

During the workshops, the students shared their thoughts and feelings about being in Canada, their first impressions of the country, their memories of home, the challenge of learning English, and the difficulty of living in a society where they were not proficient in its primary language. They told stories of their families and of their adjustment to school, and of the teasing and bullying they endured. They shared their regrets, hopes, and plans for the future. Workshops were video- or audio-taped and the stories told in them transcribed.

The director also put out a call for written stories from ESL students, and many ESL teachers sent in their students' stories and poems to the theatre. Additionally, the group had access to a collection of writings of ESL students from one school district.

At the end of the research period, the two had amassed 143 pages of material that included transcripts of interviews and young people's writings. This written document became the basis for the play.

As well, the director hired a musical director. In a project like this, it is impossible to overestimate the value of a good and dedicated musical director/composer.

Stage Two: Playbuilding and Actors' Research

During rehearsal sessions, the actors spent much of the time working as writers and directors. In addition, time was made available for actor training, which included voice, singing, physical warm-ups, games, and exercises. These activities have been documented only in instances where they were used as a way to create material.

WEEKS ONE TO FIVE

The group plays "getting to know you games" and does some informal singing with the musical director before being presented with two large pieces of paper. The first has the heading, "I know this about immigrants"; the second, "I feel this way about immigrants." The director asks the actors to write their responses to the lines on each page. When everyone has recorded their comments, the director tacks the papers to the wall where they are easily visible.

At this stage, the director noted that the group's knowledge of immigrants was predictably superficial, with such cliché observations as "they come from poorer countries," "they are glad to be in here " and "they should learn either English or French before they come." This technique is useful in recording the group's knowledge and feelings about a topic, and can serve as a catalyst for discussion.

The director and the actors discuss the comments. Some healthy arguments ensue, especially those centring on the topic of language. Some actors tell stories of students who huddle together speaking their own language in school hallways. This is something that annoys most of the actors, and they are vocal about the issue.

At this stage, there was little point in trying to make the actors understand what it is like to be unable to speak the prevalent language of a society. She listened to their comments, and noted that she had to design some experiences that would enable the actors to understand this experience.

After the discussion, the director tells the actors that they might find it interesting to look at these comments in a few months, once they have spent more time exploring the stories of immigrants.

The actors are given a copy of the stories and poems collected by the director and her assistant. The director tells the actors to read the stories at least ten times. They are given time in rehearsal to begin their reading.

Creating Scenes from Quotes

While the actors are reading, the director reviews the two charts. She selects quotes from the statements written by the actors, and writes each quote on an individual file card. When the actors are ready, she asks them to form groups of three or four. A member of each group draws a file card randomly. The director asks them to create a scene using their quote as a stimulus. The following five scenes emerge:

1. The East Indian. A girl who befriends an East Indian girl finds that her other friends are less than supportive.
2. The New Kid. A boy who doesn't speak English is teased by his new classmates.
3. The Ignored. Two students separated by an ESL student carry on a conversation. They make a few feeble attempts to include her in the conversation before proceeding to ignore her.
4. The Taxi. A cab driver heaps abuse on his non-English speaking passengers.
5. The Parent. A parent loses a job to someone of Chinese origin, supposedly because the firm has an "ethnics first" policy.

Groups take turns performing their scene. After each performance, the director asks the audience to identify the message of the scene. The actors begin to determine and articulate their feelings about immigrants.

Transcript of the Discussion

JASON: Yes, there isn't much difference between people. They're all humans, and just because they talk differently doesn't mean. . .

COURTNEY: Or they look different. . .

JASON: That they are any different. . .

ALFONZO: We as people, as society. . . there's no difference.

JASON: Some people think they are part of a club or something, you know like the white club, or the Indian club and then people categorize them.

HUGO: Yeah, stereotyping. What I think is that you shouldn't stereotype people because everybody is so unique. You know, you have to just get to know them on an individual basis, one to one, to know about how they really are. If you don't like them, that's okay.

SARAH: Yeah. You can't say I hate all certain types of people, you have to get to know them.

COURTNEY: That scene was quite stereotypical, because we think of those. . . Punjabs as taxi drivers, but I am sure that many of them that start out as taxi drivers move up in life.

TANYTH: COURTNEY, that is stereotyping. Do you think that all taxi drivers come from the Punjab? That's not true.

COURTNEY: I don't know. Don't they?

At this stage, the scenes were naïve and revealed a superficial understanding of issues. They did, however, stimulate necessary discussion. In order to go forward, the actors had to sort out their feelings and come to grips with how little they knew of the subject: they needed to see the importance of further research. The discussion also drew them into thinking about what it might feel like to be an immigrant, with little knowledge of English.

At the end of the first week, the director asks the actors to interview an ESL student. They are to tape the interview and bring the transcription of the interview to rehearsal over the next two weeks. Two actors, who are ESL students, can write their own stories if they wish.

For most of the cast, talking with an ESL student was "a first." On the whole, these students were not part of their world. As one of the actors said during the discussion, "We don't have any problems with ESL students at our school. I mean, no one makes fun of them or anything. We just ignore them." She offered this as a positive comment, not realizing that it can be a problem if one is always ignored!

Viewing Films

At the start of the second week, the actors view and discuss two films that document the stories of immigrants from a variety of countries. Following the viewings, the actors discuss what they have seen and write their responses. Here are samples of their responses:

"It is unbelievable how hard it is to immigrate! I feel so sorry for those poor people who are rejected. It is like a dream being destroyed."

"I found this film very depressing. You almost need to be perfect just to get an 'audition'. I find it sad that so many people deserve the chance but so few get the opportunity to immigrate."

"Watching this film is pretty amazing. We just don't think about how many people will give anything to be part of our country. This film has shown me how very lucky I am."

"I never thought about how much an immigrant has to go through to get here. I just thought you could just get on a plane and you're here."

"I can only think of my grandparents, who came here as peasants, with nothing to recommend them but a willingness to work hard. I don't think they'd get in today. I guess it is true, timing is everything."

"The questions the potential immigrants were asked fascinated me. I wonder what questions were asked in 1905 at the height of immigration."

"I feel so upset when they tell the people that want to immigrate that they can't come. I guess I understand that they can't let everyone in though. I never realized how many people want to come here. I just take things for granted, all the things I have that other people want."

The films were an eye opener for a group whose members had

little knowledge of the government's immigrant selection pro-
cess. Also, with the exception of an actor from El Salvador and
an actor from Chile, the group had no knowledge of the living
conditions people experience in countries torn apart by war.
During the discussion, the two actors related first-hand
accounts of living in countries in which soldiers and war are
the order of the day. These actors were a valuable resource for
the rest of the group.

Training the Actors to Conduct an Interview

Actors report that they cannot conduct effective interviews.
The director takes time to discuss this matter with the group.
Together, they decide that they should group their questions
under the following headings:

MEMORIES OF YOUR HOMELAND
- What do you miss most about your home country?
- What is your country like?
- How does your old country differ from Canada?

FINDING OUT
- How did you find out you were leaving?
- How did you react?

THE JOURNEY
- How did you come to Canada?

ARRIVING
- What were your first impressions of your new home?
- How did you find the people?
- What was your first impression of your new school?
- What are the differences between your old school and the
  school you attend now?

GENERAL
- Do you have special stories about being an immigrant that
  you would like to share?

There is discussion on the mechanics of asking questions that
elicit more than "Yes" or "No" answers. The director urges
the actors to ask "real" questions, that is, questions which they
want answered, not questions to which they already know the

answers. The director also talks about the value of silence. She tells the actors that asking another question, simply to fill up a silence, can disrupt an interview. The group is given time to practise interviewing one another. They appraise peers' techniques and provide them with feedback.

If you want your actors to conduct good interviews, they will need guidance, training, and practice. Learning how to ask the right question is key to any interview.

Creating Monologues

The director asks each actor to create a monologue that is based on one of the stories originating from the interview transcripts brought in to date. The actors are free to use the whole story, or to use various sections. Whatever method they choose, they must use some of the words of the interviewee. They are given twenty minutes for this task. At the end of this period, they present their monologues to the rest of the group. Monologues are based on interviews given by students from the following countries: Greece, Holland, El Salvador, South Africa, Mexico, Kenya, and Chile.

The director is not pleased with the monologues, which seem to owe more to television than to real life. Characters are stereotypical, and are usually poor people who are going to make it in their new country through hard work. She voices her concern to the actors, and hopes that future activities will give the actors needed insight into their characters.

The third week opens with the actors sharing their observations of ESL students in their schools and their interviewing experiences. The director notes that the group tends to interview students from predominantly European backgrounds, for example, Greek, Italian and Spanish, while largely avoiding interviews with Asian students, even though they make up the majority of ESL students in the area. She confronts the group with this observation and a heated discussion follows. Some actors state that they are uncomfortable with Asian students who "stick together and talk their own language." They feel excluded. One actor states that these students should be made to speak English.

The director believes that despite the actors' exposure to immigrants and their stories, they do not have an "in the bones" understanding of what it might be like to be an ESL student. Although they are not openly hostile or racist, the actors resent the fact that some ESL students speak their first language, and fail to understand why these students don't integrate more easily. With the assistance of a drama colleague, the director plans a role drama that aims to shift the actors' thinking through experiencing an environment in which their language is not understood.

The director explains to the actors that they will be using a technique called role drama. In this application, the director will take a role in the drama as will another adult colleague, who is subsequently introduced to the group. The director explains that everyone will role play a number of young people who are similar to the actors. Although they are not clear as to what is expected of them, the actors agree to trust the director and her colleague.

In order to increase the actors' understanding of how it feels to be an immigrant, the director planned a role drama where the actors would role play young people like themselves. In the role play, the actors have to come to terms with moving to a new country because their father has been offered a better job there. They don't want to move, but have no choice in the matter. To focus the actors and build their belief and commitment, it was necessary to build some sort of family life before they immigrated.

BUILDING A FAMILY THROUGH STILL IMAGE

The director asks the actors to work in pairs with someone who can role play a brother or sister. Actors must decide their age and what relationship they will share with their partner. They create a still image or snapshot that says something about themselves and their relationship. The snapshots are then looked at individually and read by the rest of the group. Some of the things the group sees are close relationships, sibling rivalry, and extreme differences in siblings (e.g., a "good" sibling and a "bad" sibling).

Still image is one of the quickest and most useful ways for actors to begin to project their thoughts into another character and his or her relationships. Having a still image read by the rest of the group enables actors to think about the relationship between characters and the power of body language. This provides new ideas and possibilities for the group. The exercise should be done in the spirit of "listen to what the group says about you and your sibling and think about what they are saying" rather than "guess what we are trying to show you."

OVERHEARD CONVERSATIONS

The director asks the actors to lie on the floor near their siblings and to close their eyes. They are in bed and almost asleep when they hear their mother and aunt start to talk. The director and her colleague talk in role as the mother and aunt. Their conversation, overheard by the actors, is as follows:

MOTHER: Look, I just don't know how I am going to tell the kids, okay?

AUNT: I really don't think it is anything to worry about.

MOTHER: What do you mean, it isn't anything to worry about? I'm the one who has to sit down and explain this to them.

AUNT: I think you're making too big a deal out of it, and I also think you're being too negative. This is very important to Jim.

MOTHER: Oh yes, I know. It's really important. It's important to all of us. But he's the one who has already left, and I'm supposed to somehow get the kids together and explain to them that they are leaving. I just don't think I can do that.

AUNT: People say that Sidoni is a very nice country, and there are certainly business opportunities there for Jim.

MOTHER: We'll all have to learn to speak Sidonian! Why couldn't he just leave us behind and go on his own?

AUNT: You don't mean that.

MOTHER: Why do we have to pack up and leave just because he has a better job and a so-called better life? No one speaks English over there, right?

AUNT: Jim needs your support. You and the kids are very important to Jim. What he is doing now, he needs to do and he needs you to help him.

MOTHER: What about me? I don't want to go over there. I have to leave stuff behind. What about my furniture? And what about the pets? The kids are going to go crazy when I tell them we have to leave the pets. I don't want to go!

In role, the actors share their perceptions of what they heard with their siblings. They keep their voices low so their mother and aunt can't hear them.

This exercise put the actors firmly into the shoes of these young people. In role, they began to experience what this situation would be like.

LOOKING AT THE MOTHER'S POINT OF VIEW THROUGH IMPROVISATION

The director asks the actors to remain with their partner. One partner will assume the role of the mother; the other partner, the role of the child. The actor role playing the mother tries to break the news of the move to the child. The actor role playing the child reacts to this news in the way the actor thinks she or he would in life. Most of the children are upset – some parents are able to soothe their children, most cannot.

In role drama, parts should never be assigned on the basis of gender. In this instance, both male and female actors role play the mother. We have often found that males will readily take on female roles, particularly if you explain to them that at this stage, you want them to think and not necessarily act as the character. Thankfully, in all types of theatre, the practice of males playing females and females playing males is gaining more acceptance.

DISCUSSION

Stepping out of role, the director calls the group together and asks them to discuss the improvisations. Actors role playing the children report feelings of resentment, fear, and sadness. Despite this, they experience a small sense of excitement. Most are annoyed with their parents for making these decisions without consulting them. Actors role playing the mothers report difficulty in telling their children that they must move, and most admit that they don't want to go to Sidoni.

From her research, the director knew that the majority of ESL students had these same feelings. In most cases, they were not consulted about leaving, and sometimes even the wives weren't consulted. Fathers frequently told the families after the decision had been made. Although the actors had read this in the transcripts, they were now experiencing on a first-hand basis the emotions of many ESL students. *This experience, despite its fictionalized context, brought home to the actors some of the hardships their ESL peers have experienced. This is the strength of role drama.*

PREPARING TO LEAVE – IMAGING THE ROOM AND MAKING DECISIONS

The director informs the actors that they will leave their home country in two months' time. She tells them that they must discard many of their possessions – they will only be allowed to take a few items when they leave.

With their eyes closed, the actors image their room. The director asks them to imagine themselves in the room, sitting or lying in their favorite place. They run their eyes over their room and watch themselves start to sort through books, mementos, and toys. They sort their possessions into two piles. The first pile comprises items they must keep at all costs; the second, items that can be discarded.

Imaging their room helps to make the fact of leaving concrete. One's life must be made more compact. For teenagers, who often have a tendency to be collectors, this can be a difficult task.

The director asks each actor to write a letter in role to his or her best friend who is away on holiday. In the letter, actors explain the situation and express their feelings about leaving.

Writing in role is a powerful tool for deepening understanding of other people's behavior and thinking. Actors must project themselves into this context and think and write as that person.

A PRECIOUS POSSESSION

The director has the actors visualize one object they cannot leave behind. The object, which may have little or no practical or monetary value, is something that the actors prize above all other possessions. They visualize the object and think of why it is so valuable. With their partner, the actors share their "precious possession" and the reasons why it can't be left behind.

Actors sit in a large circle. They take turns introducing their partner to the group, describing their precious possession, and explaining why they must take it with them when they leave.

This was a moving exercise. That all group members had thought deeply about their possessions was obvious. The possessions ranged from heirloom jewelry that had been handed down through generations through old pictures of best friends and favorite ripped jeans.

NARRATING THE GROUP THROUGH THE JOURNEY

The group sits on the floor while the director narrates them through the journey.

"Finally the day comes for your departure. You are on the plane, probably feeling a mixture of emotions. It is a long journey and you have lots of time to think. However, there are things to amuse – movie and audio channels and no doubt many of you have taken your own music. You think about some of the things you have left behind and wonder when you will see your friends again. Perhaps you have pets that had to be left behind. You wonder too about Sidoni, what it will be like, what things might be familiar. You sleep some and then fourteen hours later you look out of the plane and see Sidoni beneath you. How will you describe it in letters to friends back home? How are you feeling as the plane taxis toward the arrival gate?"

On finishing, the director allows a few minutes of silence.

ARRIVING IN SIDONI

The actors imagine that they have just arrived and are waiting in the baggage hall for their luggage. It was a long flight and people are feeling many emotions. The director asks the actors to freeze in a still image that shows a group of immigrants waiting for their luggage. When the group is frozen, she enters as a guide saying:

"Welcome to Sidoni. I know it has been a long flight and you are very tired. You need to go into immigration now. I hope that it won't take too long, but you know government departments. Unfortunately, I must leave you as I have to attend to another group. Now, if you'll take your bags and just go straight down the hall to immigration. . ."

The group picks up their baggage and proceeds down the hall. Here they are met by the director's colleague, in role as an immigration officer. She speaks gibberish to them. The group is surprised! Making no sense, she explains that she wants them to form three lines – men, women, and children. There is much confusion and frustration on the part of the actors, who cannot comprehend what she wants. The immigration officer speaks louder and tries to indicate what she wants them to do non-verbally. Most of the actors appear dismayed. With no warning, the director moves them straight into the next setting of school.

SCHOOL

The director explains that they have been in the country a month and are now ready to start school. Because they don't speak the language of Sidoni, they are to be enrolled in a Sidoni as a Second Language class. The drama colleague has set up a "classroom," complete with pictures and captions printed in "Sidonian." The actors are asked to take their place in class. The drama colleague, in role as the teacher, begins talking gibberish to the actors, pointing to the pictures and encouraging them to say gibberish words. The actors' reaction is classic – they are baffled. One student asks if the teacher speaks English. In gibberish, the teacher answers, "Nona Anglasisa." The students understand her and many grow silent.

As the lesson progresses and it becomes clear that they are not going to hear their own language, the actors exhibit many of the same behaviors witnessed in ESL classes. Some try hard to learn, some make derogatory comments about the teacher, some talk to each other in their own language, and some retreat inward. A small percentage begin to get up to mischief, one boy switching the words under the pictures while the teacher's back is turned. The teacher is enthusiastic and is trying to teach the class to the best of her ability. The lesson continues for twenty minutes before she assigns a task and leaves the room. The students immediately hold a class meeting. One boy tries to get the others to behave and attempt to learn the language. The others boo him. A rather raucous ten minutes passes. One of the students says, "We aren't ever going to learn this language!" At that moment, the director steps in and ends this part of the role drama.

WRITING

The director calls the group out of role and asks them to write about how this exercise has made them feel. The writing speaks for itself. Here are some comments taken from the actors' pages:

"I realize for the first time how important my language is. I felt so frustrated and annoyed when she was talking to us in her language. It was the pits."

"I wanted to hide and just block reality."

"I tried, I really did, but in my head the syllables kept getting mixed up and I had no idea what was going on."

"I always see kids learning English and I never knew how they felt. Now I know."

At the end of the writing period, the actors read aloud their comments. A lengthy discussion ensues. The main consensus arising out of the talk is that the actors, for the first time, realize what it may be like to arrive in a country where one does not speak the language and has not come there voluntarily.

For the director, this was a turning point in the play's creation. She felt that the role drama had provided the actors with the experience they needed to begin to step into the shoes of ESL students. They were beginning to understand the realities of living in a new country.

At the beginning of the fourth week, the director gives the actors time to re-read the transcripts. She instructs them to find a story that interests them and that lends itself to presentation. The actors work in small groups of five or six. The groups choose the following three stories.

THE BIRTHDAY

I found out that I was coming to Canada from Singapore the night before my thirteenth birthday. That kind of lent a little downer to my birthday party. This was the first birthday that I had a party. We went to a restaurant called the Noodle House and acted a bit crazy. My friends put ice down my back and I thought I'd get back at them later. We had fun. I didn't think about it at the time, but now I have all my birthdays alone in Canada.

THE BOMB

I remember the saddest thing that ever happened to me. It was when I was living in Nicaragua. Some of my friends were playing in a vacant lot and two of the kids found a bomb. You see, after the revolution of 1979 there were a lot of unused bombs that got buried and people didn't find them until later. These kids were only ten years old and didn't really know how dangerous it was. Some of the kids dared them to rub it with a stick or they were chicken. So one of the boys rubbed it with a stick and it exploded and he died. Luckily the bomb had lost a lot of its original strength or it would have blown up the entire town. The boy was blown to pieces.

THE GIANTS

The first day I arrived in Canada was a nightmare. I couldn't believe how tall the Canadian men were. They were like giants. I asked a man, "Where's the toilet?" He didn't understand me. So I looked up at him and said, "Excuse me sir, where's the toilet?" I've really got to go!" He laughed, and pointed down the hall, so I went. When I went into the toilet, I saw two ugly teenagers. Their hair was like chickens, only green! I didn't know if they were boys or girls! I just stood there, staring at them. I didn't know what to do, so I just stared at them. They said, "Bonjour" and I didn't know what they said so I just said "Bonja" and I ran out the door.

The director works on the Giants scene with the group. Together, they decide to present the scene in story theatre style. In this form, one person narrates as well as acts. The rest of the group plays both characters and scenery. A great deal of physical experimenting takes place as it is decided that there has to be two "giants" because of the line, "I couldn't believe how tall the Canadian men were, they were like giants!" Giants are finally created by two of the smallest actors sitting on the shoulders of taller actors. They are now ten feet tall! When the scene is finished, the actors write it up in rough and the director takes it away to complete. The finished scene is as follows:

The Giant Scene

BOY: The first day I arrived in Canada was a nightmare. *(Actors move into positions to make up the environment. On stage left, there is the airport hall with people putting luggage onto trolleys, and people greeting each other and saying goodbye. The environment is frozen, so as not to take focus from the actor. On stage right, there is a door and a toilet.)*

> BOY: I couldn't believe how tall the Canadian men were. *(In the background, four actors make up the giants and move downstage until they are level with the boy who turns and looks at them.)*
>
> BOY: They were like giants! I asked a man *(turns to address the giant),* Where is the toilet? *(Giant shrugs.)*
>
> BOY: *(to audience)* He didn't understand me, so I looked up at him and said, *(he addresses the giant)* Excuse me sir? Where is the toilet? I've really got to go! *(He crosses legs, and generally makes wanting to go to the toilet gestures. The giant laughs.)*
>
> BOY: *(to audience)* He laughed and pointed down the hall, so I went *(Actors make a hallway. Giants move upstage. The boy runs down the hallway and arrives stage right at the toilet where two "punks" are smoking. The boy enters the toilet and then stops dead when he sees the punks, who are frozen, ignoring him).*
>
> BOY: *(to audience)* When I went into the bathroom, I saw two ugly teenagers. *(Teens turn to audience with annoyed looks.)* Their hair was like chickens, only green! I didn't know if they were boys or girls! I just stood there staring at them.
>
> TEENS: *(to boy)* Bonjour. *(The boy stands staring. The teens offer the cigarette.)* Bonjour!
>
> BOY: I didn't know what they said, so I just said, "Bonja." *(The teens collapse laughing.)* And I ran out the door! *(He runs out.)*
>
> *End of scene.*

The musical director/composer, who has taken part in all of the rehearsals, presents two songs to the group in the fourth week. "Changes" is a poem written by a fifteen-year-old Korean boy, which appears in an anthology. The musical director sets it to music, and it becomes a lyrical song with many harmonies. The rap song comprises verses created from the words of ESL students. The group is asked for input into the lyrics, and some changes are made to the rap as a result of their suggestions.

At this stage, the director was satisfied that they now had two great songs and one scene together. Also, in discussion with the musical director and the cast, she had chosen the monologues she thought should be in the play. The director scripted these up so that they could be presented to the actors at the next rehearsal.

WEEKS SIX TO TEN

The director tells the actors that they are to try to set the beginning of the play. This will be a series of monologues written by the ESL students that tell of their memories of leaving their country. The scripted opening monologues are presented to the actors, and they choose the monologue they would like to present. The actors are given fifteen minutes to create their monologue.

The director tries a variety of approaches:

1. All actors are on stage and are spread across it. The actors begin their monologues together so that the audience only hears snatches of them.
2. The actors, still scattered across the stage, begin their monologues singly, with the next actor beginning before the person preceding him or her has finished. When the second person begins, the first actor lowers his or her voice until it is scarcely louder than a whisper. Actors try this several times, and the musical director underscores.
3. The actors huddle upstage and come forward one at a time with an individual monologue. Each actor leaves the stage as the next actor begins. In a variation of this, the actors stay on stage after they have finished their monologue.

Although these were interesting experiments, both directors felt they were too abstract to be of value.

The director talks to the cast about these approaches, and suggests that the play needs a context. The musical director asks the question, "Where are these people?" and responds to his own question by saying, "At the moment they could be on the moon!" The director suggests that the play be set in the context of a school. The opening scene could take place in the school hallway, which is typically the social hub. It is here that teens "mark out their territory," friends exchange gossip and news, members of the opposite sex cruise each other, and allegiances are made and broken. Here, in this daily jostle of friends and enemies, outsiders are readily apparent. The "rap song" seems to lend itself well to this atmosphere. The actors are enthusiastic about this idea, and the director scripts this up for the next rehearsal.

The draft of the script now looks like this:

A bare stage. Music underscoring begins. Enter three students who go to their lockers. They establish lockers and then freeze as the first actor begins his monologue. The monologues are to be the thoughts inside these young people's heads. They are the memories they carry with them.

ACTOR: In Vancouver, when it is grey and raining
       I think about Greece a lot
       The whiteness of the buildings
       The clear, blue water
       The red poppies in the Spring.

ACTOR: El Salvador was hot. . .

While these actors are speaking, the rest of the cast arrives on stage, and freezes at the lockers. The rest of the monologues continue until the last one.

ACTOR: I finally told my mother, I hate English and I'm not going to back to school!

The school bell rings. The hallway explodes into life, students greet each other, check on homework, etc. A boy pushes an ESL student out of the way.

Rap Song:

The play has a beginning!

IMPROVISING NEW MATERIAL

The session begins with a discussion about incidents of racism, teasing, or bullying the actors have witnessed in their own school settings. Lists of ideas are made and recorded on chart paper. Working in small groups, the actors improvise scenes to show and discuss together. The scenes include:

- a teacher reprimanding a group of kids who have been teasing an ESL student. This makes it worse for him, not better.
- a group of students being racist with an ESL student, calling

him names and shoving him around. It ends in the student being beaten up by the mainstream students.

- a group of mainstream students pretending to be friendly to an ESL student and coaching him to swear under the guise of teaching him ordinary words.

The actors show and discuss the scenes. The swear word scene appeals to them because they recognize from experience and from the story transcripts that this is a common experience for ESL students. The actors are aware, however, that this play will be performed for elementary school audiences so swearing on stage is inappropriate. The group returns to the transcript to find stories about swearing. There are quite a few. An example from the transcript follows:

Swear Words Story

When I came to school in Canada, I learned swear words very fast, because the kids in my class came up and taught me. They say, "F. . ..K you" and I didn't know they were swear words, and so I said "P. . . off" and "F. . ..k you!" After I said those words one of the girls whispered to me, "Don't say those words, they are swear words." My face was turning very red. I thought the teacher was listening and I would get into a lot of trouble.

The director sets a task for the actors. She asks them to form three groups to create a scene that expresses this idea without using words that would be inappropriate for an elementary school audience. The groups work on this task, but on the whole are not very successful. One scene that almost works involves a group of students teaching an ESL student names for parts of his body. They teach him that the word for his forehead is penis. In the scene, the boy develops a headache and, clutching his forehead, tells the teacher, "Please Miss, penis hurt." The scene is hilarious, but in discussion the actors insist that you could never say a word like penis in elementary school. They maintain that the audience will be so embarrassed they will shriek and scream. The actors tell the director that since swear words are commonplace, they would be accepted by the students, if not by the teachers! The problem is left unsolved.

The director points out that in her reading of the transcripts she has been struck by the number of times ESL students have said that they were not going to return to school and they weren't going to learn English because the experience was too frustrating. She asks the group, "What do you think would happen if one of these young people went home and said that to a parent?" The group has a number of ideas. The director asks them to work in pairs to create a scene where a child confronts a parent and says, "I'm not going to learn English and I'm not going back to school!"

The pairs work on this while the director circulates, helping when asked and providing directions in terms of staging. Three interesting scenes emerge and are discussed by the entire group. The ESL students in the group give valuable insight into how they think an immigrant parent would react to this rebellion in light of cultural expectations. The group has much to ponder. The director asks the actors to write up these scenes for her as she thinks there should be a scene like this in the play and she wants to work from their ideas. With their partner, they write up the scenes and give them to her.

It is important to have a record of things that you think need to be in the play.

It is essential to record what happens during a playbuilding session, especially when working with beginners. Often, a scene is improvised and you think you can replicate it. Because of the spontaneous nature of improvisation, however, the scene usually changes. Sometimes that is for the better, but often the original spark of the scene is lost and the new scene doesn't work as well. Having a record of it is the only sure way to avoid this problem. In this project, a professional video production was being made and most of the work was captured on video. Despite, this, actors still wrote out the scenes.

The director asks the actors what stories from the transcripts they think should be in the play. Actors agree that these stories should be included:

- The girl from El Salvador, who was so traumatized by arriving in Canada that she locked herself in her bedroom and would not come out, even for food. Her mother took her meals on a tray each day and left them at her door. This continued for months.

- The boy from El Salvador who saw his high school friend shot at random by soldiers.
- The Korean girl who explained how to get a boyfriend in Korea.
- The African student who was forced to read aloud from her school text which used the word "nigger."
- The student who escaped with his family through the "killing fields" of Cambodia.

The director talks with the actors about the problem of having too many sad stories in the play.

A finished play is like a painting or a piece of music. Overuse of the same note, color, or texture is boring and ineffective. A play that is relentless in its sadness loses its audience. To be successful, a play should be both entertaining and thought-provoking. It should have the power to make the audience laugh, cry, and think of its message even after they have left the theatre. Because this play was shaping up to be very dark, the director looked for some humor. The stories chosen by the actors were powerful, but overwhelmingly sad. Material was needed to provide balance.

STAGING THE RAP SONG

The director has the actors form groups in which they will brainstorm events that happen around lockers and in the school hallway during breaks, and before and after school. When they finish brainstorming, each group picks three to five of their images that they think could be used in the opening rap song. Actors show the other groups their images, and each group is given part of the song to incorporate into a freeze frame. The groups are frozen until they say their line.

Although these freeze frames would not necessarily be used in the play, they provided the director with a series of images of life in the school hallway. This information would help her when the song was staged. The young actors knew this territory well, and it was interesting to watch them depict the subtleties of relationships and events in the hallway. Having the actors show these events in still image gave the director a rich source of material to work from and allowed the actors to contribute ideas. This is the creative partnership at its best.

The rap song is staged. At the end of the rap song, the director wants an actor to bang locker doors, one after the other. She knows that this will sound like gunfire, and thinks that this could trigger memories for young people who had lived in war-torn countries.

Unfortunately, there will not be a set as such for the play since it is a touring show. One actor suggests that bursting a paper bag would give a similar effect. They try the suggestion, which becomes the bridge from the rap song into the war monologues.

The director now needs a bridge from the war monologues into the airport scene. She has the actors work in groups to create short improvisations that will establish an airport. These are to be done fairly quickly and written down for the director. She, in turn, will write a short airport announcement to bridge into the scene. This scene becomes:

- an announcement. Canadian Airlines announces a delay in Flight 426 to Calgary, Winnipeg, and Toronto. Would passengers on this flight please report to the Canadian counter?
- a series of quick scenes that could happen in an airport.

The script had now progressed to:

A bare stage. Music underscoring begins. Enter three students who go to their lockers. They establish lockers and then freeze as the first actor begins his monologue. The monologues are to be the thoughts inside these young people's heads. These are the memories they carry with them.

ACTOR: In Vancouver, when it is grey and raining,
      I think about Greece a lot
      The whiteness of the buildings
      The clear, blue water
      The red poppies in the Spring.

ACTOR: El Salvador was hot...

While the actors are speaking, the rest of the cast arrives on stage and freezes at the lockers. The rest of the monologues continue until the last one.

ACTOR: I finally told my mother, I hate English and I'm not going to back to school!

The school bell rings. The hallway explodes into life, students greet each other, check on homework, etc. A boy pushes an ESL student out of the way.

Rap Song:

A paper bag is burst. A boy falls to the ground as if he is being shot at. All the students look. Pause.

STUDENT: What a geek!

Actors laugh and walk away. They freeze. The boy gets slowly to his feet and begins his war monologue.

WAR MONOLOGUE ONE: We were in Science class when the tanks came. . .

WAR MONOLOGUE TWO: The only safe place from the bullets was under the bed. . .

WAR MONOLOGUE THREE: When we heard the gunshots, we just froze. . .

Airport scene:
Canadian Airlines announcement.
Three ten-second scenes establishing the airport.

The Giant Scene

One fact that emerges from interviews with ESL students is how many feel torn between old and new cultures. Typically, these students describe the struggle as "being on a tightrope" or "being pulled apart." Some groups report having to live in two separate cultures. At home, they behave quite differently from school where they often try hard to fit in with the other students. The director conceives a scene where the actors will be engaged in a tug o' war, with an ESL student caught in the middle. She takes the words of the tug o' war from some of the ESL students' transcripts.

• Don't lose your cultural roots, speak Chinese.
• Just tell your parents you are your own person!
• You'll be a doctor, we're proud of you!

- How are you going to learn English if you are always speaking Chinese with your friends?
- If you can't speak English, you'll never make it in Canada!

It seems a logical step to place the song "Changes" directly after that.

Here, the director and musical director were making writer/ director choices. Sometimes the actors have input into this, and sometimes these decisions are made by the director. She or he should certainly seek the group's advice if stuck. You can say, "I've got this idea. It may be stupid, and I'm not sure if it will work. What do you think?" This gives actors the opportunity to reject your ideas without damaging your ego. Actors are often only too willing to tell you when they think an idea is stupid and can often come up with a much better one! At this stage, however, the play was beginning to flow, and the actors and directors liked what was happening.

During the last week, the director works on creating a scene. She uses the previously improvised idea about students who go home and confront their parents with the fact that they aren't going to learn English or go to school any more. These two scripted scenes are presented to the actors for discussion and workshopping during week eight. Time is spent on creating the illusion of a tug o' war without a rope. The whole group tries out the parent/child rebellion scene with combinations of mother/daughter, father/daughter, father/son, and mother/son. The scene is confrontational with the last line belonging to the child who says, "I'm not going to school and I'm not learning English!" The group experiments with different reactions: the parent freezing in the act of hitting the child; the parent storming out and leaving the child; the child storming out; the parent taking the child in his arms. This last choice works well in combination with the father and daughter pairing. The actor playing the father is one of the more mature actors of the group and the child is the youngest actor in the group. They are convincing as a father and daughter. They end up being cast in this scene in the final play, with the sympathetic ending. It works very well.

At the time of writing, the play has been done with six different casts in Canada and Australia. Given the right chemistry between the actors, all combinations work.

Because the play is going to tour to schools, the director and actors decide to use a story theatre approach for staging the scenes. In this way of working, the actors stay on stage at all times and make environments for the scenes. They become lockers in hallways and desks in classrooms.

The director took a calculated risk here. She knew that it would work well for the more light-hearted scenes, but was worried that the convention of having actors become scenery for more serious scenes could cause laughter. However, she decided to go ahead with it to see what would happen.

The director gives the actors four stories that she thinks should be in the play. They are: "So Small" (a humorous story about a five-year-old who, on looking out of the window on arriving in Canada, is amazed that the people are so small), "My Room Was Canada" (the story of the girl who locks herself in her room and won't come out), "Are You a Virgin?" (a story of a girl with limited English who answers "No" to the question "Are you a virgin?"), and "Canada Clothes" (a story of a girl who is dressed by her grandmother to prepare for Canada's cold).

In small groups, the actors translate these stories into story theatre style. The director, using the ideas presented by the actors, scripts them with only a few minor alterations, and they are played almost word for word from the transcripts. Time is spent making environments for the scenes, and these are inventive and interesting.

Particularly interesting was the bedroom created for "My Room Was Canada." This environment always caused "oohs" and "aahs" from the audience when five actors became a bed, complete with cover and pillow. The audience held their breath when the actor lay down, but they never laughed at the scene which was both poignant and moving.

The secret of having effective environments is to train the actors to be neutral when they become inanimate objects. The audience accepts that they are cupboards, walls, chairs, and beds as long as these objects aren't winking, smiling, or moving. Of course, if there is a funny scene, it is sometimes great fun to have objects that express amazement or amusement. In this instance, however, humorous scenes would have been inappropriate.

The director decides to present a scene titled "Second Generation" to the actors. The scene, which she had developed previously with a group of elementary school students, centres on a group of friends. When one of the girls brings a friend into the group who cannot speak English, the others are not pleased. Despite the fact that these girls are second-generation immigrants, they show no understanding of the ESL girl's feelings. The scene ends with them telling their friend to "get rid of her," and give her an ultimatum, "It's us or her!" The actors discuss this scene and express the opinion that it should be in the play.

The musical director has now completed two more songs. One, "Scarecrow," was inspired by ESL students who have written on the theme of loneliness. The musical director uses many of their phrases to create a song that tells of the loneliness of being a stranger in a strange land. It is an instant hit with the actors. The director thinks that it would be a perfect song to follow "Second Generation."

The musical director's second song is an attempt to solve the problem of showing how ESL students often learn four-letter words before any others. He creates a witty song in which four-letter words are spelt out.

This is presented to the actors for comment. They are firm in their belief that this is unacceptable for both elementary and secondary school students. He sets them the task of making it more acceptable. In groups, the actors take up his challenge and change the lyrics to:

Say the "F word," it means "Can you help me?"
Say it again, it means "Hello,"
"Bonehead" is the teacher's name
And "up yours" means "thank you."

The play has now been seen by over 120,000 elementary and secondary school students across Canada, the U.S.A., and Australia. There has never been a complaint about this song.

In week nine, work continues on the individual scenes and on creating the environments. The director has now reached the point where she must take the scenes, songs, and bridges and order them into a script. Outside of rehearsals, the director works as a writer, creating a first draft of the play that can be read by the actors. The musical director works on a finale song.

At the beginning of the tenth week, the director presents an almost complete draft script to the actors. She asks them to discuss the script, and to provide her with feedback.

She believes that another upbeat scene is still needed. She asks the two ESL actors if they have a fun story or moment that they can share with the group. One of the boys tells a story about how he wanted to ask a girl out, but was reluctant to because he didn't speak English very well. However, he gathered his courage and, as he told it, "I got the girl." The director takes the idea and writes the "She Likes You" scene.

In this scene, an ESL boy pines for a girl named Maya. Two of the school's more macho males notice this and set him up to play a fool. The boys tell the ESL student that Maya likes him. They convince the boy to approach her as they snigger in the background. The great joke backfires on the two boys when Maya agrees to go out with the ESL student. He is jubilant, the macho boys are incredulous. The scene ends with the boy calling out, "Thanks guys!" while the two chase each other with a view to inflicting physical pain.

The director feels that this is the perfect final scene because of its upbeat nature. A finale song will complete the play.

This scene is always a hit, especially with school audiences. Frequently audience members cheer.

The musical director reviews the draft and thinks that a song should be inserted between "Canada Clothes" and "My Room Was Canada." The group discusses the fact that many of the ESL students commented on Canada's cleanliness. One student thought that there must be cleaners who were cleaning the cities all night! The group returns to their transcribed interviews to review interesting passages they had marked previously and which had not been used in the play. A comment that was made in several interviews focused on the use of phrases such as "You're welcome" and "Have a nice day." In most instances, we do little more than mouth these words. The musical director takes those ideas and writes the song "Dear Papa."

Sample Verse – Dear Papa

Well Papa, it's been about a week
I'm learning how to speak
And I've been out to see what I can see
And what a sight!
The trees are always green!
The streets are always clean!
They must be out there scrubbing all night long
And no dirt can be found
Especially on the ground.

Chorus
Good day. Hello. How are you?
Goodbye. And have a nice day.

by John Sereda

In the Australian production, this song was dropped and a new song about coping with Australian slang was inserted.

WEEKS ELEVEN TO FIFTEEN

The musical director presents the group with a finale song, "I'll Be All Right," in which ESL students express their hope for the future. The group rehearses the "She Likes You" scene, creates environments, and changes actors so that everyone has a chance to play in this scene. After discussion, it is decided that the last song will take place at the lockers again. With this in mind, the director stages the finale song.

The director completes the script in week twelve and brings it in for the group to read. Several readings are done, with different people assuming different roles. A reading is completed with the songs inserted. Everyone is pleased with the final script. The play's synopsis is as follows:

- Opening monologues: Thoughts of home.
- Rap song: ESL students ask the question, "Where do I fit in?"
- War monologues: Students from Vietnam, El Salvador, and Uganda talk of their experiences.
- At the airport.
- Scene: The Giants. An Asian boy finds the Canadian men "like giants." In the airport washroom, he encounters two punks. He has never seen anything like them before.

117

- Monologue: Canadian Clothes. A girl's grandmother dresses her in clothes suitable for the Arctic. The girl arrives in the middle of the summer and swelters.

- Song: "Dear Papa." ESL students sing of how clean and green Canada is and how everyone seems so friendly, but it is just a veneer.

- Scene: My Room Was Canada. A young ESL student locks herself in her bedroom for months so she will not have to deal with being in Canada.

- Scene: English Is too Hard. A child rebels against learning English.

- Scene: Tug-o'-War. A non-naturalistic scene where an ESL student struggles with keeping her own culture and accepting the new one.

- Song: "Changes." The lyrics, originally written as a poem by a fifteen-year-old Korean boy, tell of his difficulty coping with the changes he experienced as an immigrant caught between cultures.

- P.E. Scene: This was a bridging scene created by the director to take the group into a new situation where lots of things could occur simultaneously. A small immigrant boy is continually pushed aside at the basketball hoop. The other boys complain that he is useless because he is so small. This triggers a memory of his arrival in Canada as a five-year-old, and forms a bridge into the next scene and song.

- Scene: So Small.

- Song: "Ha, Ha Very Funny." In this song, mainstream students teach a newcomer some words that he does not realize are swear words. He says them to the teacher and gets into trouble. The other students think this is very funny.

- Virgin monologue: A young girl talks of her embarrassment when, not understanding, she answers "No" to the question, "Are you a virgin?"

- Scene: Second Generation: Two girls, children of immigrants to Canada, are particularly insensitive to a newcomer from India.

- Bridging scene: The group is at the lockers again. A boy arrives with a snowball announcing that it is snowing outside.

- Snow monologue: An ESL student describes the first time she saw snow. She likened the snow to white bird feathers falling from the sky.

- Scene: She Likes You. An ESL boy is inadvertently helped by two macho boys.

- Bridging scene: It is the end of the day and the students pack up at their lockers. Three small positive monologues are given on: (1) the helpfulness of an ESL teacher, (2) a boy's experience of war and how these experiences are a part of him, and (3) a student's ambition and determination to make it in his new country.

- Finale song: "I'll Be All Right Someday."

Stage Three: Rehearsal and Performance

The play is cast and put into rehearsal. Because the entire group has been involved in its creation, the play is ready for performance after twelve hours of rehearsal.

7

Assessment

Many teachers struggle with the question of how drama can be assessed. Some have been reluctant to formally assess creative work, feeling that as it involves the whole person assessing is in some way judging the student rather than a particular set of skills. However, assessment in drama in general and playbuilding in particular must be done for there is a perception in schools and the wider community that work that cannot be assessed is not important. Playbuilding involves students in relevant and meaningful learning experiences and, as ongoing assessment is part of other subjects, teachers directing playbuilding owe it to their students to find a way to assess and evaluate their work.

What Is Assessment?

Assessment involves collecting data and making judgments about student achievement. It is important to ensure that the data we collect and the judgments we make are useful, not only to the school and parents, but also to the students.

Collecting data may be done in a variety of ways and by using a variety of tools. This may include observation, interaction, work samples, and logbook reflections.

Observations may be made at both informal and formal levels, and may be recorded as anecdotal records or notes. Interactions may also be informal or formal, and may include conversations, discussion, debate, and conferences with an individual or with a group of students. Work samples may include written samples of students' reflection, aesthetic responses, writing in role, script or synopsis writing, or visual aspects such as design, running orders, lighting plans, and cues sheets. Logbooks comprise ongoing reflections that record an individual's or a group's response to the development of the work. Logbooks or journals can provide a rich source of information about the processes that individuals have gone through in developing a playbuilt play.

Assessments in drama can be made by an outsider, by someone interacting in the process, and by the participants. In each case, different aspects will be assessed for different data and from different viewpoints. Assessment by an outsider can be made through observations that encompass watching the work in progress, as well as the work in performance. In Australia and England, engaging an outside assessor is common practice in Drama and Theatre at senior levels.

Assessments made by interacting can also involve an outsider, the teacher, or the students' peers. Self-assessment usually involves the keeping of a logbook or some process of either oral or written reflection.

All forms of assessments are equally valid. They provide different kinds of information about students' achievements and, taken together, provide a clear picture of their progress in aesthetic, cognitive, sensory and physical, and social learning areas of playbuilding.

Observations by an outsider provide a distanced audience response to either the work in progress or the performance, and give information that focuses on the social, aesthetic, and ensemble aspects of the work. Self-assessment deals with personal and subjective responses that cannot be tapped in other ways. It is through this means, particularly if a logbook or written reflections are taken into account, that the outsider has access to students' inner thoughts and feelings. Together, these assessment modes provide a more comprehensive picture of the outcomes of the activity than that of any single measure.

Judgments about data collected for assessment may be made against particular criteria (criterion-referenced assessment), or by ranking performances against one another (norm-referenced assessment).

It is important to bear in mind that despite their appearances these are not objective processes. Any judgments made by human beings are, of necessity, subjective. We need to acknowledge this subjectivity, and then seek to minimize any unfairness that may arise from this by using a range of judgments and a variety of assessment tools, and by clearly establishing the parameters of the judgments to be made.

Criterion-referenced assessment involves establishing specific criteria and measuring the students' achievements against these criteria. Ideally, the criteria should address specific, observable learning.

Norm-referenced assessment poses a dilemma for the drama teacher because it involves ranking students against one another. Due to the heuristic nature of the activity, this is problematic. Our assessments are as much concerned with how meanings are made as with the meanings themselves. It is difficult to take this into account in norm-referenced assessing, which relies heavily on outside observations to maintain validity and reliability.

Assessing Playbuilding

Assessment in drama/theatre studies enables the teacher to monitor the development of the playbuilding process, and to make adjustments to ensure greater achievement. It also provides information to the students that is useful in directing future learning. A mark of 9/10 tells a student very little, whereas an assessment that points to particular achievements on specific criteria and suggests areas for further work is most useful.

Assessing playbuilding involves collecting data and making judgments about the *process* of development of the play and its *product*, that is, the playbuilt play in performance. It is important that these two aspects are kept in focus. The kind of data that can be collected during the process of development of playbuilding differs from the kind of data that can be collected during the performance of the product.

During the process of development of a playbuilt play, students work to build an ensemble, and interact with peers and the teacher in different ways than those witnessed in a performance. The audience, or an assessor who sees only the performance "on the night," has a different view of what has been achieved. While this view is limited in the sense of not encompassing the process, it is also a view that those engaged in the process cannot access, precisely because it is the view of an outsider.

Current moves in assessment tend to take into account what can be done rather than what is known. This move towards competencies or skills can provide a useful focus for the assessment of the playbuilding process and product.

A variety of skills or learning areas are developed during the playbuilding process. These may be categorized in various ways, such as:

1. Aesthetic learning. Understanding of the art form that allows students to make aesthetic judgments.
2. Cognitive learning. Involves thinking skills such as concept formation, critical and analytical thinking, and logical and lateral thinking. Cognitive learning encompasses all language codes – verbal and non-verbal.
3. Sensory and physical learning. Concerned with ways in which the senses develop and heighten perception, and those processes that involve control of various aspects of the body.
4. Social learning. Involves learning that students make about themselves and others. Through working in theatre, students develop a sense of self and a sense of group membership. They expand their world views through interaction and the work itself. In some ways, social learning, coupled with aesthetic learning, are the most significant areas of learning in the playbuilding process. Social learning, however, is difficult to assess, particularly when an objective or numerical value has to be assigned.

In devising an assessment program, it is important to make decisions about:

- what to assess
- when to assess
- who will assess
- how to assess

It is also important that you do not overassess. Making decisions about criteria is the first step.

Establishing Criteria

Outlined here are ways in which criteria might be established for the types of learning that occur in a playbuilding activity. As well, suggestions have been included regarding ways in which data may be collected through the process and at the performance. When these assessments occur will depend to a large extent on the nature of the project and the particular requirements of the educational institution.

Aesthetic Learning

- Understand and develop a range of drama forms, including:
  — role,
  — improvisation,
  — storytelling.

An outsider or the teacher can observe students at work and determine their ability to identify roles within the playbuilding context, to research a role, and to develop a role in performance. Peer assessment, in the form of reflections or discussions, can provide an interactive perspective on the development of role and of the use of elements of drama.

Work samples are useful in providing data about students' development of a role, particularly work samples that show this development over a period of time. These samples include written or performed work, and might be recorded on video to enable comparison of the development over a period of time. Written work samples could include writing in role, writing outside role, and reflecting on the role.

Self-assessment tools, such as logbooks, will also provide useful information about the development of role.

- Explore and use a variety of dramatic and theatrical conventions to refine dramatic action, including:
  — tension,
  — symbol,
  — focus,
  — contrast,
  — style,
  — movement/stillness,
  — sound/silence.

An outsider or the teacher can observe ways in which students use particular techniques to explore a play's issues. Observations can be made regarding how the students use artistic elements to create scenes, non- naturalistic pieces, monologues, still images, and so on.

Interacting through discussion, debate, and directing the work provides the most reliable information about this aspect of the process.

Peer assessment and self-assessment tools will also provide useful data for making judgments about how the students have met this criteria.

- Establish a relationship with the audience.

Observations of the audience provide an important source of information about this criteria. An observer can note the ways in which the audience responds to each performer, and to the performance as a whole. In some situations, it may be possible to have direct feedback in the form of an actors' forum at the end of the performance.

Interactions with the students/actors in a debriefing session will also provide information, as will logbooks or reflections of individuals.

Cognitive Learning

- Research a theme, issue, concept, image, or idea.

An outsider or teacher can make observations of the range and appropriateness of the information sources the students have used, the way in which they used these sources, and the quality and usefulness of the information in shaping the theatre piece.

Students can keep logbooks that document their research process, make written reports about the research and their own conceptual development, and provide work samples that evidence the sources and how they have used them, for example, interview records and script excerpts.

Discussions within the group can be observed or documented to provide evidence of how the group has responded to the research and development process.

Sensory and Physical Learning

- Refine expressive and performance skills.

An outsider making observations of the rehearsal process and the ways in which students work to develop skills in performance provides the most useful data for this criteria.

There are no easy "tick-a-box" ways to assess playbuilding skills. It is also not necessary to assess every aspect of learning in any one playbuilding activity. The assessment should be viewed in the context of the course's ongoing assessment. This allows the teacher to target particular aspects of the learning for assessment, and assists the students in focusing their learning activities.

Where playbuilding is part of a broad course of learning, either in drama or Theatre, English or Social Studies, the activity can be targeted for assessment in a way that is both useful for the students' ongoing learning and for making judgments and reporting to the wider community. This can be achieved by establishing specific criteria for the assessment of the process and the product. Where specific criteria are used, it is important that the students and the wider community be aware of the criteria that have been applied in each case.

A typical pattern of assessment might involve data collection throughout the playbuilding process with judgments being made at specific points, and at the performance. This would include the collecting of work samples and peer assessment by way of student interaction. Self-assessment would involve a review of logbooks and oral and written reflection.

Social Learning

- Collaborate, contribute ideas, work with the ideas of others in the group, and perform as part of an ensemble.

An outsider can make observations of the interactions within the group process, taking into account how members interact with one another, whether they make contributions to group activities and explorations, and whether they work with the contributions of others in the group.

Peer assessment will provide useful information for assessing criteria that cannot be easily accessed in other ways.

Logbooks and oral and written reflections will also be useful in tapping into the experiences of group members in relation to their interaction and ensemble work.

An outsider may observe interactions between the performers as they present the playbuilt play to an audience, noting the nature of the ensemble as a working/performing group.

Reporting

This sample of assessment criteria also provides a useful framework for reporting student achievement to the wider community. By addressing these criteria in a report and outlining the nature of student achievement, it is also possible to "educate" the wider community as to the nature of the learning that takes place in drama/theatre and particularly in playbuilding.

Appendix

Glossary

chorus: group of actors who speak or sing in unison.

didactic theatre: theatre that has as its intention the making of a statement or the teaching of a moral or political viewpoint. Often, this is achieved through the use of alienation techniques.

designer: person responsible for the overall "look" of the play. The designer's job is to ensure that the costumes and set are authentic to the period and make a statement that fits in with the general concept of the play. If lighting is used, the designer is responsible for ensuring that the lighting adds to the mood of the play.

director: person responsible for the interpretation of the play. She or he co-ordinates all aspects of the play, including acting, designing, lighting, and costumes. The director plans and conducts rehearsals.

dramaturge: person who collaborates with the playwright and director, and who is responsible for researching, translating, or reshaping the script during the rehearsal and production process.

empty chair: technique in which an empty chair is placed in front of the actors who are to imagine that the chair is occupied by a character. The group asks the character questions, and anyone in the group may answer in role as that character. It is a technique that allows everyone to play the central character, and is also an effective means of gaining more information about a character.

flat: timber frame generally covered with canvas that can be used as scenery, or as a device actors use for entrances and exits.

focus: element of drama which ensures that the dramatic action is clearly framed and communicated to the audience.

freeze frames: series of linked depictions that are presented to an audience to demonstrate key issues in a dramatic moment.

hot seat: process where actor assumes the role of his or her character and fields questions from other actors.

intertextuality: reference to other texts through allusions or through direct quotes.

mood: feeling or atmosphere created by the dramatic action.

non-naturalistic scenes: scenes that do not attempt to replicate real situations, but use a variety of non-naturalistic devices to express ideas and issues, for example, machines, sound-scapes, and movement pieces.

on-stage audience: actors on stage are the audience for other actors who are performing to them, all of which is viewed by the real audience. The on-stage audience acts as a kind of commentator for the real audience.

props: objects or items that are used in the course of dramatic action. Props may sometimes take on symbolic significance.

role drama: a Canadian term to describe situations in which a director assumes a role. In the U.S., it is called process drama. In Australia, it is referred to as group drama. It was pioneered as a theatre form by Dorothy Heathcote and Gavin Bolton.

rhythm: rate and pattern of movement and timing in a scene.

sets: physical stage configuration that establishes the setting for a scene in a play.

silent negotiation: actors do not discuss what they are about to do, but "negotiate silently." As an example, a group is creating a still image using silent negotiation. One member of the group steps forward and puts his or her body into a position that expresses something about the topic. The rest of the group observes, "reads" the image, and then silently adds to it by joining the member.

sociogram: diagram that represents the relationships between characters.

soliloquy: conversation between an actor alone on stage and the audience.

soundscape: use of sounds, words, or sentences by a group to create mood or shed light on a character, situation, or event.

still image: also called still photo, tableau, and depiction, it involves the group creating a still image or photo of an event or moment in time that can be read by the audience.

symbol: gesture, object or action, or a visual, verbal, or auditory image that takes on significant meaning.

tension: created through relationships, action, ceremony, mystery, and surprise. Tension is the key element of dramatic performance.

theatre form: shape and structure of the play on stage.

theatre-in-education: type of didactic theatre that aims to teach within the context of the classroom.

Bibliography

General Drama Books

Bedford, W. 1990. *More "Life Be In It" Games*. Sydney, NSW: ABC Books.

Bolton, G. 1992. *New Perspectives on Classroom Drama*. New York, NY: Simon & Schuster, Inc.

Booth, D., & C.J. Lundy. 1985. *Improvisation*. Toronto, Ont.: Harcourt Brace and Company.

Charters, J., & A. Gately. 1986. *Drama Anytime*. Rozelle, NSW: Primary English Teaching Association; Portsmouth, NH: Heinemann

Haseman, B., & J. O'Toole. 1990. *Communicate Live!* Port Melbourne, Vic.: Heinemann Education.

Michaels, W. 1990. *Played Upon a Stage*. South Melbourne, Vic: Thomas Nelson Australia.

_____. 1995. *Played Upon Shakespeare's Stage*. Sydney, NSW: Shakespeare Globe Centre.

Neelands, J. 1990. *Structuring Drama Work: A Handbook of Available Forms in Theatre and Drama*. New York, NY: Cambridge University Press.

Swartz, L. 1995. *Dramathemes: A Practical Guide for Teaching Drama*. Markham, Ont.: Pembroke Publishers; Portsmouth, NH: Heinemann.

Tarlington, C., & P. Verriour. 1982. *Offstage: Elementary Education Through Drama*. Toronto, Ont.: Oxford University Press.

Role Drama Books

Booth, D. 1994. *Story Drama: Reading, Writing, and Role Playing Across the Curriculum*. Markham, Ont.: Pembroke Publishers.

Davis, L. 1989. *Drama K-6: Stepping Into Role*. Sydney, NSW: Department of School Education.

O'Neill, C., & A. Lambert. 1982. *Drama Structures: A Practical Handbook for Teachers*. London, UK: Hutchinson & Co.; Portsmouth, NH: Heinemann.

Saxton, J., & N. Morgan. 1987. *Teaching Drama*. London, UK: Hutchinson & Co.; Portsmouth, NH: Heinemann.

Tarlington, C., & P. Verriour. 1994. *Role Drama: A Teacher's Handbook*. Markham, Ont.: Pembroke Publishers; Portsmouth, NH: Heinemann.

Verriour, P. 1994. *In Role: Teaching and Learning Dramatically*. Markham, Ont.: Pippin Publishing Ltd.; Portsmouth, NH: Heinemann.

Playbuilding Books

Bray, E. 1992. *Playbuilding*. Sydney, NSW: Currency Press; Portsmouth, NH: Heinemann.

Matthew, S. 1989. *Getting into the Act: Communication Through Drama*. Wellington, NZ: GP Books.

Sklar, D.J. 1991. *Playmaking: Children's Writing and Performing Their Own Plays*. New York, NY: Teachers and Writers Collaborative.

Books on Questioning

Morgan, N., & J. Saxton. 1994. *Asking Better Questions*. Markham, Ont.: Pembroke Publishers.

Assessment

MacRae, K. 1984. *Drama in the Classroom*. Sydney, NSW: Department of School Education.

Graham, N. and J. George. 1992. *Marking Success*. Markham, Ont.: Pembroke Publishers.

Index